Too Stressed to Think?

Too Stressed to Think?

A Teen Guide to Staying Sane When Life Makes You CRAZY

by Annie Fox, M.Ed.,
and Ruth Kirschner

edited by Elizabeth Verdick

free spirit
PUBLiSHiNG®

Helping kids
help themselves™
since 1983

Library of Congress Cataloging-in-Publication Data
Fox, Annie, 1950–
    Too stressed to think? : a teen guide to staying sane when life makes you crazy / by Annie Fox and Ruth Kirschner.
        p. cm.
    Includes index.
    ISBN 1-57542-173-9
1. Stress in adolescence. 2. Stress management for teenagers. I. Kirschner, Ruth. II. Title.
    BF724.3.S86F69 2005
    155.5'18—dc22   2005018484

At the time of this book's publication, all facts and figures cited are the most current available; all telephone numbers, addresses, and Web site URLs are accurate and active; all publications, organizations, Web sites, and other resources exist as described in this book; and all have been verified as of June 2005. The authors and Free Spirit Publishing make no warranty or guarantee concerning the information and materials given out by organizations or content found at Web sites, and we are not responsible for any changes that occur after this book's publication. If you find an error or believe that a resource listed here is not as described, please contact Free Spirit Publishing. Parents, teachers, and other adults: We strongly urge you to monitor children's use of the Internet.

Associate editors: Jennifer Brannen and Al Desetta
Cover design: Marieka Heinlen
Interior design: Percolator
Illustrator: Marieka Heinlen

10 9 8 7 6 5 4 3 2 1
Printed in the United States of America

Free Spirit Publishing Inc.
217 Fifth Avenue North, Suite 200
Minneapolis, MN 55401-1299
(612) 338-2068
help4kids@freespirit.com
www.freespirit.com

Dedications

To David, my rock and my pillow, always in all ways, thank you for 31 years of love and partnership. —A.F.

To my parents, Leona and Philip Kirschner, who always encourage me to realize my dreams. —R.K.

Acknowledgments

Many thanks to all the students whose voices guided our thinking and writing. Robert Sapolsky, Ph.D., was called on at the outset for advice, and we thank him for his time and expertise, for his wit, and for his inspired work on the subject of stress. Elissa Epel graciously reviewed our early brain material. Jennifer Brannen at Free Spirit Publishing brought a clear and curious mind to this manuscript at the beginning of the editing process. Thanks especially to our editor, Elizabeth Verdick, who brought it all together and took it across the finish line. We are very grateful.

Annie: A big thank you goes to Hey Terra's teens online and in the real world. You and your questions are my teachers. To sweet Sarah, thank you for being my surrogate daughter. And to my own Fayette and Ezra, thanks for choosing me as your mom and always showing me what really matters so I can stay balanced. You two honor your dad and me with the choices you make.

Ruth: Thanks to great colleagues Tessa Gaddis, Elizabeth Greene, and Kate Northcott who encouraged me at crucial junctures in the development of the workshops. Their readiness to engage in lively exploration of ideas has been a prompt, a help, and a joyful mix of ongoing enthusiasm, intellectual passion, and personal wisdom—how lucky I am in these friendships. Marin Country Day School was the place where my ideas for the "Stress and Ethics" workshops took shape. Without this great school's alliance in the early stages of the program, this book would not exist. Most of all, to my daughter, Lucy, thank you for inspiring me to stretch my understanding of so many things. You teach me something new every day.

Contents

Part 3:

Taking Care of Yourself (Because You're Worth It) **125**

Introduction

Overloaded. Overworked. Overwhelmed. We've all been there. Some of us (maybe you?) feel like we practically *live* there.

Suppose you're asked, "What's the number one stressor in your life?" At any time of the year (except summer), you'd probably answer, "School!" When we talked to and surveyed more than 1,000 teens for this book, that's what most of them said. It's also what almost 50 percent of the 9,500 teens who took the online Teen Stress Survey at About.com said when asked, "What's your biggest source of stress?" The teens reported that family problems ranked second, with 17 percent of the votes. Dating and relationship issues came in a close third at 16 percent.

But whether it's school, getting over a breakup, or constant arguments with parents, it can all feel like the same thing. Because, in a way, it *is* all the same thing: *stress.*

Stress is part of life, and most people believe there's nothing you can do about it. You might think you already know so much about stress that you could write your own book on the subject! So, why have we bothered writing this book, and why should you bother reading it? Because stress creates lots of problems—the obvious ones (like fights or frustrations) and the ones you may not be aware of (like what's actually occurring in your brain and what happens to your body if you have too many pressure-filled days). We want to help you deal with those issues, so you can stay strong and grow up healthy. We also wrote this book because we've learned that most teens need some help learning how to de-stress and live more balanced lives.

Balance—have you thought much about it? Most of us don't. It's not until we're *off*-balance that we notice. Try this out: Stand up like you normally do—your body is naturally balanced, your spine keeps you upright, and gravity does its part. You know you're not going to fall over, and so you feel pretty much at ease. But if you pick up one foot and try to stand still, you may feel a little unsteady. The higher you lift your foot, the shakier you get. Now keep your foot up and lean all the way to one side—what happens then? You wobble and probably worry about falling. As you feel yourself losing your balance, you automatically right yourself by spreading your arms and putting your foot back down. With both feet planted firmly on the ground again, you begin to relax.

What does this have to do with stress? Stress is like losing your balance, except that it happens internally. And because you're not actually in danger of falling over, you don't have an automatic reflex action to right yourself. So, there's nothing protecting you. When stress starts building up inside, you're not as steady as you were before. Sometimes, you may not even realize how unbalanced you've become.

In our work with teens in classrooms, workshops, and online, we meet a lot of young people who say they're stressed and confused. Whenever one of them asks us, "What should I do?" we say, "The first thing is to calm down. Get back in balance just a bit, so you can begin thinking more clearly about your options for getting help and resolving your problem." In other words, even righting yourself a little can help. But there's more you can do—and that's what this book is about.

We created a curriculum called "Stress and Ethics" to help teens learn more about the effects of stress and how to get back in control of their thoughts, feelings, and choices. The book you're reading now was inspired by that curriculum and by the many teens we've talked to and learned from. We work with teens every day because we care about you, and we want to help.

As parents, we've come to understand that you and other teens are in transition—definitely not children anymore but not yet adults. You're experiencing all kinds of changes— physical, emotional, intellectual—and change can be stressful. Add to it the fact that we live in a fast-paced world

that seems to be speeding up steadily. Speed increases pressure. Nobody likes feeling pressured, but hardly anybody's slowing down. Everybody's always busy. No time to just do nothing. No time to breathe.

At a pace like that, some people start to believe that their success is measured by their schedule and how much they can pack into a day. Does that sound familiar? Maybe the adults in your family think that way—or maybe you do. Either way, this can lead to unrealistic expectations about what you should be getting done and whether it's enough.

Even if you don't always realize it, you might be stressed out for much of the time that you're awake. And during those hours, you make all kinds of choices—small ones, like what time you're going to start your homework, and big ones, like what's right or wrong for you. Making good choices requires clear thinking, and guess what? You can't think clearly when you're stressed. No one can. If you're making choices without thinking, then what are the results? Well, possibly mistakes, problems, and more stress.

Put simply, when you feel pushed and pressured, you may not make the best choices for yourself. The key to avoiding a lot of hassles in life is to first understand what's going on in your brain and in your body that may prevent you from thinking clearly during times of stress. Once you understand that, you can learn to better manage your stress so that you feel balanced and centered more of the time. Sounds like a good thing, doesn't it?

With practice, you can learn how to stop a stress response as it's happening and avoid making decisions you might later regret. But this book will teach more than stress-relief techniques—you'll also discover how to:

- understand yourself better and respect what's important to you
- recognize the pressures you're under and how to face them with greater calm and confidence
- trust that you can deal with problems and challenges
- make conscious choices that are more in line with who you really are

- create a more manageable schedule so you can relax and enjoy being a teen (you deserve it!)
- get yourself back in balance whenever you feel off-center
- create and maintain healthier relationships with the people in your life, now and in the future

Each chapter of this book includes activities and supporting tools for you to try, not just once but as often as you need them. In addition, you'll find quotes by real teens we surveyed or corresponded with online; we hope their words will show you that you're not alone. We've also included stories of teens facing challenges, dealing with problems, and learning to manage the stress in their lives. Maybe you'll see yourself in some of these stories, or perhaps you'll discover that some of the tools presented might work for a situation in your own life.

Some people believe that books find their way to you when you're ready to learn something from them. Maybe you've picked up this book because you're ready to change the way you deal with stressful situations. We hope our book will help you understand yourself better so that you can deal with stress in a healthier way and be happier.

Although you can't control the behavior of others, you've got 100 percent control over your own behavior and that gives you enormous power. Your choices matter—they make a difference. So, you've got to choose wisely. The first step on this journey toward having a more balanced life and making good choices begins with understanding what's going on inside you. Ready?

In friendship,
Annie and Ruth

P.S. If you want to write to us about this book, please get in touch with us care of Free Spirit Publishing Inc., 217 Fifth Avenue North, Suite 200, Minneapolis, MN 55401-1299. Or email us at help4kids@freespirit.com. We promise we'll write back.

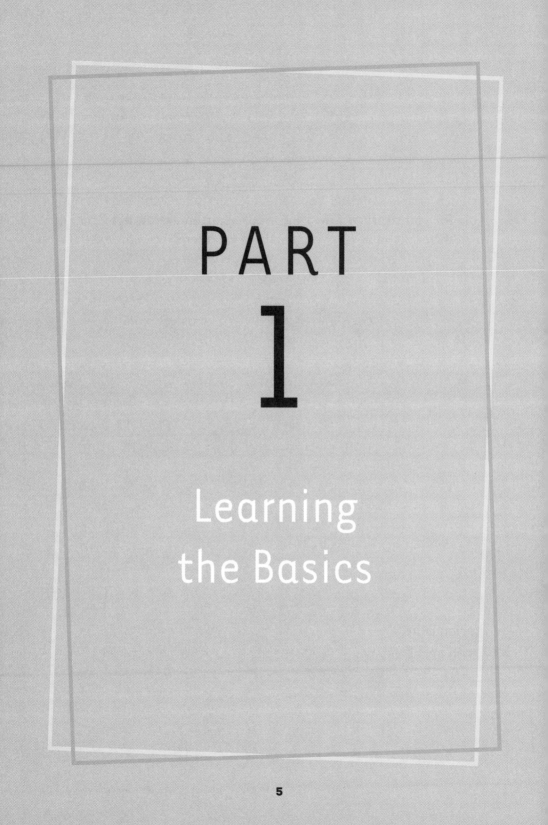

PART
1

Learning
the Basics

1

Stress 101

KAT'S best friend, Emily, was acting weird but wouldn't tell her why. Kat was worried, and she really wanted to help. Finally, Emily said she'd talk if Kat promised not to tell anyone what was going on. Kat promised, and Emily confided something really private that she didn't want anyone else to know. Kat said the secret was safe with her.

But a few days later, their other friend, Maria, asked Kat what was wrong with Emily. "She's been so quiet and moody. I'm worried about her." Kat confessed that she knew what was up but couldn't tell anyone. Maria pressed her, saying that if Kat really cared about both her and Emily, she'd talk. Kat felt confused, like she couldn't think straight. "Fine, I'll tell you, but you have to promise this goes no further." It wasn't long before Emily learned that her secret was out. She felt betrayed; Kat felt simply awful.

MIKE was hanging out with some of the guys, playing video games and laughing about stuff that had happened at school that day. When one of his friends told an offensive joke, everybody laughed except Mike. He thought the joke was kind of sick and stupid. Mike lost track of what was happening in the game he was playing. He wanted to say something to his friends—but what? He tossed aside the game controller and announced, "I don't feel like playing anymore." But he wouldn't tell his friends why.

So, what were Kat and Mike thinking? Well, they weren't thinking, at least not clearly. Stress makes it hard to think—that's true for anybody.

Even though your brain is operational 24/7, you don't always use it effectively. How come? It's not because you're stupid, clueless, or a teen. It's because stress has an effect on your brain. It's very difficult to stay calm and in control when your stress response has been triggered.

Q & A

What does the word <u>stress</u> mean to you?

"Like everything is pushing you, and you don't know what to deal with first."
—Charlene, 15

"It means that you have so much on your mind, and you can't get it out."
—Debra, 11

"Pain and failure. Nothing's right."
—Evan, 13

"Stress is a terrible, clawing anxiety."
—Max, 13

"It means I'm nervous about something, and I can't concentrate on anything, and I usually feel sick."
—Keisha, 14

"A burden of things that bother you."
—Steven, 14

"To me it means tired, worried, angry, and fed up."
—Aaron, 14

"Stress means never feeling like you can relax. You always have to be doing things that you feel forced into."
—Lisa, 14

"Stress means having a bad day or agonizing over stuff that plagues you, because you are in a situation where you can do little to fix it or can't fix it as fast as it needs to be fixed."
—Raymond, 16

"Stress is when you are doing too much already and anything else would make you bust."
—Michelle, 16

"Stress is thinking about so many things at once that my head hurts, and I can't focus on a single thought or task."
—Kate, 18

"Stress is a tax on your soul."
—Kory, 14

What is stress, anyway?

Stress is definitely a word you hear a lot, but what does it really mean? We define it as:

what happens to your body when it's faced with demands and pressures of many kinds. It's a push you feel inside that throws you off-balance (mentally, emotionally, and physically), often making it hard to think clearly or make good decisions.

That off-balance feeling usually doesn't come from just one source but from many. Some of the sources are external, meaning outside of you—like school, friends, bullies, parents, or difficult social situations. Other sources come from within—for example, when you feel sick, or you're in pain, or you have strong emotions that you're not sure how to handle. The result? A stress response starts inside you, shoving you out of your comfort zone where things are usually just fine (a state known as *equilibrium*) and into a whole other place that's sometimes pretty uncomfortable.

Although stress changes how you feel, that's not always a bad thing. Some stressful moments can actually be exhilarating, like when you're playing the last two minutes of a tied game, or you're up on stage singing a solo or giving a speech. At times like these, you're yanked out of your comfort zone and you have to face major pressures—and, sure, stress is a part of that. You may feel off-balance but also pumped up and excited. The extra pressure can give you the edge you need to do your best.

And what about that tingly feeling you get all over when someone you've been crushing on finally asks you out? Or when you've just been told that you won something awesome—like a contest or a school election? Or when you're falling head over heels in love? Inside, your heart pounds, you feel shaky, and your thoughts begin to race—and you're totally off-balance. (But who's complaining, right?) You've shifted out of your ordinary experience to a level of heightened awareness. That can make you feel focused, full of energy, and alive with possibilities.

Then there's the other kind of stress—the kind that weighs you down and makes you feel moody and mean, like it's all too much to deal with. People react to it differently: Some grumble and complain; others look frantic and freaked out. Some may withdraw from family and friends; others might scream and yell. How *you* react depends on who you are, where you are, and how you feel at the moment.

For example, seeing your ex-girlfriend with another guy might be devastating today, but two months from now when you have a new girlfriend, who cares? Or, suppose your teacher announces a chemistry test for the end of the week. While you're in class, surrounded by friends who are all in the same boat, you may not feel overwhelmingly stressed—yet. But later that night, as you look over your textbook, you could feel a lot differently. Your head might race with thoughts like, "I'm totally going to fail!"

When your switch gets flipped, a stress response is triggered. Your head may fill with doubts or with memories of other times when you felt stressed or in danger. Often, these thoughts whirl out of control and just keep coming. Not surprisingly, none of this helps you get ready for your test or whatever else you're facing.

No one likes feeling overwhelmed. But often, we don't know what to do to feel better. It's safe to say that most of us *want* to feel better, if we could only learn how. This book is all about managing stress—but before you can start managing it, you've got to understand it. And that means first getting familiar with life's most typical stressors.

Meet the four stressors

Put simply, a stressor triggers your stress response. There are four major kinds: environmental, physical, emotional, and psychological. You don't have to memorize them—just get to know them. You won't be tested on this!

1. Environmental: These occur outside of you but have an effect on how you feel inside and out. For example, when:

- a sudden rainstorm leaves you soaking wet at the bus stop
- air pollution hurts your eyes and makes it hard to breathe
- extreme cold or heat affects your comfort level
- loud music hurts your ears, making it difficult to concentrate
- a crowd jostles you or seems to be closing in on you
- traveling in dangerous weather conditions puts your safety at risk
- neighborhood violence makes you feel scared and unprotected

Depending on where you live or what you do each day, you may come into contact with noises, smells, bad weather, traffic, crowds, rude people, or other forces beyond your control. These stressors often feel like an indirect hit that throws you off-balance.

2. Physical: These are more like a *direct* hit. For example, say you trip and fall on your face—that's a physical stressor. Or suppose you wake up with the flu, and you feel like you've been rolled over by a tank. Or maybe you're irritable but you're not sure why, and then you remember that you haven't eaten or even slowed down for a drink of water. Physical stressors may be mildly annoying or go so far that they take a major toll on your health, depending on their severity and your reaction to them. Examples:

- itchy or sunburned skin
- lack of sleep
- thirst or dehydration
- extreme hunger
- illness, injury, or pain
- burnout

3. Emotional: These are unexpected pressures that leave you feeling confused, surprised, upset, hurt, angry, or even excited. You're thrown off-balance, you don't know where you stand, and you're not sure what your next step should be. For instance:

- changes in routine (a new class schedule or after-school activity)
- other people's behavior (someone who never paid attention to you before starts noticing you)
- unwanted changes to your appearance (a bad haircut, weight gain or loss, zits)
- special recognition (you win an award, and everyone makes a fuss)
- a bad grade (this is especially difficult when you studied hard and expected to do better)
- technical difficulties (the computer you're working on crashes, or you can't get access to the Internet)
- disappointments (like when you lose a competition or a friend lets you down)
- scheduling conflicts (you've been invited to two cool events on the same day, and you have to choose one)

- losses (when a friendship comes to an end, you break up with your boyfriend/girlfriend, or you get cut from a team)
- fights (with family members, friends, or boyfriends/girlfriends)

Although these stressors can be tough to deal with, they only last a short while, and soon you regain your balance once again.

4. Psychological: These stressors stem from *unresolved* emotions (for example, something's been eating you up inside, maybe for months or years, but you haven't known how to deal with it). Feelings of anger, fear, sadness, regret, or shame seem to move in and make themselves at home inside you. Maybe they stick around so long that you barely remember where they came from or what your life was like before things got so difficult. Psychological stressors can lead to, or be signs of, deeper medical issues, such as depression or an eating disorder. Some examples include:

- serious family problems (constant arguments, not being able to depend on family adults)
- social pressures (being excluded from a clique, feeling isolated)
- unresolved relationship issues (with family, relatives, friends, boyfriends/girlfriends, or teachers)
- ongoing academic troubles (poor test scores, learning difficulties)
- constant bullying or harassment

There's one other form of psychological stress: chronic worrying. Humans may not be the only mammals who worry (there is some evidence that whales and elephants worry too), but we are definitely the ones who get the gold medal! You, but not your cat, can remember bad experiences from the past and then start worrying that the same thing will happen again. As a human being, you're also likely to worry about things that have never happened to you personally but could. Or to agonize over things you "could have" or "should have" done differently but can't change now. Stress can lead to worrying, and in turn, worrying creates more stress. (For tips on coping, see page 53.)

What are *your* stressors?

A stressor always nudges, pushes, or drags you out of your comfort zone and puts you on alert. That "Uh-oh!" feeling happens right after your brain recognizes that something has just shifted and you're now experiencing physical or emotional discomfort. Good-bye equilibrium—your stress response has just kicked in.

Do any of the following stressors sound familiar to you? This is what the teens we surveyed said about the stress triggers in their lives and how they react to them.

Stressors

deadlines · multitasking · social pressures · homework · strangers · the future · personal problems · nagging · everything that has to do with school · my past · rumors · term papers · teachers · abrupt changes · loud noises · fights with friends · my health · my weight · college decisions · sports · conflict · confrontation · failure · too much work · tests · guys · girls · my ex-boyfriend · my ex-girlfriend · sex · an overloaded schedule · late buses · time-management issues · worries · new environments · overly forceful coaches · mean people · popularity · my mom · my dad · my stepmom · my stepdad · my sister · my brother · grades · expectations · rules · world events

Just as there are a variety of stressors, there are also a variety of reactions that teens say they typically have when they're feeling off-balance.

Feelings/Reactions

sad · moody · quiet · I act weird · uptight · crazy · crabby · I don't want to cooperate · I pick fights · anti-social · I feel like screaming · it's like I'm foaming at the mouth · bitchy · irritable · angry · I feel like crying · I catch an attitude · I feel like tearing things up · I swear · I cut myself · I buy more stuff · cranky · frustrated · edgy · testy · I talk too fast or too much · withdrawn · lonely · exhausted · grumpy · I hide my feelings · I get very worried · I feel disappointed in myself · I act like I have PMS · annoyed · I lash out · argumentative · aggressive · impatient · easily agitated · depressed · upset · mean · tense · very emotional · I complain · I overeat

Have You Reached Your Limit?

Check to see if you recognize any of the following emotions/behaviors, all of which can be signs of severe stress. Do you:

☐ feel irritated, annoyed, or angry most of the time?

☐ often have hurt feelings?

☐ constantly worry about big and small issues?

☐ cry frequently, without knowing why?

☐ find that you can barely eat, sleep, or get through the day?

☐ get into lots of fights—verbal or physical?

☐ often feel sad, lonely, or completely alone?

☐ take dangerous risks, like driving too fast, taking drugs, drinking alcohol, or doing other things that hurt your body and mind?

> If you answered yes to any of these, you may have reached your stress limit, which can leave you feeling continuously off-center and out of control. What can you do? Get some help. Find an adult you trust: a parent, teacher, school counselor, or religious leader. You don't have to go it alone—there are people who can and *will* help. For more tips, see Chapter 10.

You still have *choices*

Once you're stressing, who's in charge? The answer: *you*. But how can you possibly keep your balance and make good choices when you're not thinking clearly? Well, it's not easy.

One key to learning how to manage stress in healthy ways and get back on track is *recognizing that you're feeling off-balance*. Get in the habit of checking in with yourself by asking, "Am I feeling stressed right now?" or "Is this another one of those stressors in my life?" Know that you do have choices about how you react.

Everything you do is a choice, whether it's deliberate and conscious, or impulsive and unconscious. Good choices make the world a safer, more just, and less stressful place. Poor ones create stress and unhappiness, whether they affect you, your friends and family, your school, your community, or the wider world. Need proof? Just check the front page of today's newspaper for the latest bad choices people have made and their consequences. No doubt about it, choices matter.

Gandhi, the father of democracy in India, said, "Be the kind of change you want to see in the world." That's a powerful statement. It means that your choices matter—they affect not just your own life but the lives of others too. When you feel positive, calm, and balanced, you're definitely going to make better choices. In other words, you'll be more likely to do the right thing—and that can be a great stress reliever. You'll feel better and so will the other people in your life: win-win.

This book is designed to help you create and maintain a less stressful lifestyle. But you're not going to get there just by reading the chapters. Really think about what you're reading and practice being more aware of your thoughts and feelings. In each chapter of the book, you'll find tools for de-stressing and opportunities to act on what you're learning. Try them. Here's your first challenge:

 THINK ABOUT IT: What are your everyday stressors? What are your *biggest* ones? Why? How do you usually feel or react when faced with stressors big and small?

 TALK ABOUT IT: Your stressors can change throughout your life. Chat with a parent, grandparent, or someone else who has known you well since you were younger about some of the things that *used* to set you off but don't anymore. What has changed for you? Talk about what's gotten better (or worse) now that you're a teen.

 WRITE ABOUT IT: Writing is a great way to become more aware of who you are and how you behave. With greater self-awareness, you'll begin to make more conscious choices and manage your stress. Any personal writing that you do (like journaling) is private. No one should ever see what you've written, unless you choose to share it. That's why, when you write in a journal, you can give yourself permission to be totally honest. Get any kind of journal you like (a notebook, sketchbook, or blank book) and write about a personal experience you've had with stress. Did you have to make a choice? What was it? What was the outcome?

dating   jobs   family   pressure

cliques   homework   identity   tests

bullying

friends

2

Stress and Your Brain

What does your brain have to do with stress? The short answer is *everything.* Brains aren't just for learning algebra or cramming for the SATs (though they're good for those things too). Your brain is the storehouse for who you are. Even though it only weighs about three pounds, your brain is where all your memories, feelings, beliefs, opinions, dreams, fears, great ideas, and random facts (state capitals, your locker combination) are stored.

It's also the home of your stress response. All of the emotions and physical reactions you experience when you're stressed are part of this response, and your brain controls them. You can't rewire your brain to become immune to stress, but by understanding how different parts of your brain work (and don't work), you can start changing how you respond.

Your Exuberant Brain

Scientists once thought that the brain had its biggest growth and developmental spurts long before the teen years. As it turns out, that's not entirely true. Research now shows that the brain changes and develops at an incredible rate during the teen years, forming amazing new connections and pruning the ones it no longer needs. Scientists refer to this as *exuberance.*

What does this mean for you? That you're changing constantly. Your thoughts, interests, activities, and moods can shift and go in whole new directions every day. But this also can contribute to your stress level. You might find yourself being more impulsive, making choices or taking chances that don't always make sense to you later—especially when you're stressed. For better (mostly) and for worse (sometimes), it's all thanks to what's going on in that exuberant brain of yours.

Your brain: an act in three parts

Picture your brain as having three main parts. (It's actually a lot more complex than that and doesn't really come in "parts," but this will help you get the idea.) All three parts of your brain work together to make you who you are.

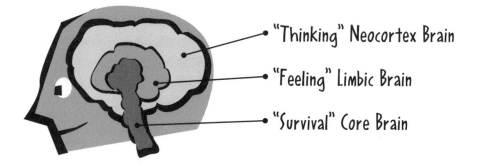

"Thinking" Neocortex Brain

"Feeling" Limbic Brain

"Survival" Core Brain

The three parts, which have developed over the course of life on earth, are:

- the "survival" or reptilian brain, also known as the core brain (which first appeared 300 million years ago)
- the "feeling" or mammalian brain, a.k.a. the limbic brain (which has been evolving for the past 50 million years or so)
- the "thinking" or neocortex brain, also called the new brain (which has been evolving for about the past 5 million years)

You need all three parts of your brain to be a complete human being. No part is better or worse than another, and each plays an important role.

Your survival brain keeps you alive day and night (and in emergencies) because it controls:

■ breathing

■ heart rate

■ body temperature

■ sleeping and waking

■ swallowing and digestion

This primitive part of your brain is kind of like your survival command center. Its functions are automatic and take place without any *thought* from you. And that's a good thing: If you had to think every time you wanted to breathe or digest food, you'd never get anything done and you'd probably be dead.

When you're stressed, this is the part of your brain that's in charge of your automatic stress response, which is designed to help keep you alive during emergencies. So, it's all about survival. Reptiles don't do email, but they've survived for hundreds of millions of years, so they're obviously doing something right.

Your feeling brain helps you store memories, care about others, and experience the full spine-tingling range of human emotion. This part of the brain developed in response to our need to form family bonds, take care of our young, and get along in cooperative groups (all of which help mammals to survive). This is also the part of the brain that reacts during moments of intense

FACT!

*Your brain actually does have a "stress central." Known as the **amygdala** (uh-mig-duh-la), it's a small almond-shaped structure that's involved in generating and responding to emotions. The amygdala is especially tied to fear, anger, avoidance, and defensiveness.*

emotion, triggering a stress response. (For example, when you
blurt out something you didn't
mean to say or trip over your own
tongue when talking to someone
you'd love to impress.) Intense or
confusing emotions can quickly
overload the feeling brain.

Your thinking brain is your
rational, reasoning brain. It lets
you explore the world intellectu-
ally, weigh the pros and cons of a
situation, and make clear, conscious
choices (like deciding to wear a bike
helmet or control your temper).
This part of the brain sets us apart
from every other creature on earth.
No other mammal, and certainly no
reptile, has anything quite like our
thinking brains. Unlike chimps or
cats or dogs, we humans can think
elaborately about our feelings, talk
about our fears and dreams, write
poetry, compose music, and make
plans for taking care of ourselves and others. We analyze, evaluate, and reflect on events, decisions, and behavior—past, present,
and future. It's too bad that our thinking brains aren't available to
us 24/7.

Why aren't they? Because when you're under stress, the part of
your brain that shuts down most readily is an area called the *pre-
frontal cortex,* which plays an important role in how you make decisions and control your impulses. So, suppose someone insults you
or yells at you, and you start to stress. Typically what happens is
this: (1) Your feeling brain overloads, (2) it triggers your survival
brain to release stress hormones, and (3) your thinking brain takes
a backseat. In other words, you stop thinking and start reacting.

FACT!

*As your brain matures
during the teen years,
certain connections,
or **axons,** thicken and
become coated in some-
thing called a myelin
sheath. This fatty sub-
stance makes the axon
more efficient and a lot
faster. It's estimated that
electrical charges (which
drive all sorts of func-
tions in your brain, from
memory to movement to
learning) travel 100 times
faster on an axon that's
covered in myelin than on
one that isn't. Think of
it as your brain's way of
switching from a dial-up
connection to DSL.*

Your stress response: it's all about survival

Sometimes stress can be a good thing—the excitement of preparing for a date or that extra energy that helps you make a great catch. Having a stress response can leave you weak in the knees, but it can also give you an amazing power surge.

In fact, your stress response is key to human survival. If you were a cave girl or a cave guy and the volcano next door suddenly exploded, sending a fiery river of lava your way, a few things would happen:

- Your heart would beat faster.
- You'd get an extra burst of energy.
- You'd run faster than you normally could.

Your stress response is designed to help you avoid danger, so it gives you the power you need to fight or run away (this is often called a *fight-or-flight response*). When the volcano erupts, you don't need to talk it over with your neighbors, form a committee, consider the options, or make a plan. You need to *run!* Instead of being buried by lava, you could potentially escape to higher ground and survive. In an emergency situation, your stress response is the best thing you've got going for you.

Do Males and Females Respond to Stress Differently?

Recent research suggests that guys and girls don't respond to stress in exactly the same way. As it turns out, fight-or-flight is more commonly a *male* response to stress. Research by a University of California, Los Angeles, scientist named Shelley Taylor and her colleagues shows that females frequently respond to stress with behavior described as *tend and befriend.* According to Taylor, women and girls are more likely to take care of themselves and their stress by reaching out to others. Why? These actions may be rooted in the need for females to protect themselves and nurture their children. So, while females *do* experience a fight-or-flight response, their levels of a hormone called *oxytocin* can help buffer the effects. That very same hormone may also encourage the behavior of talking to a friend or connecting with a group—both of which can be great stress relievers.

The truth is whether you're male or female, you may experience both fight-or-flight *and* tend and befriend. Sometimes, you might be more likely to get aggressive and physical in times of stress. At other times, you may feel like talking to someone instead. Take a look at your friends or family members—how do they typically react when stressed? Do you think it could be true that someone's stress response is rooted in his or her gender?

There are a few other stress reactions that are common too, like freezing up or freaking out (when you go on overload and can't seem to move). You can probably recall reacting like this at some point. At times like that, your stress response may feel more like an ambush than a survival mechanism.

The urge to protect yourself, run away, freeze, or hide can be helpful in *some* cases, but let's face it: In most day-to-day situations, fighting, fleeing, freezing, or freaking aren't really going to help. As sophisticated as the human brain is, it still relies on the primitive survival brain in times of stress. And that survival brain—useful though it may be—can't tell the difference between a tiger and a geometry test. When the pressure is on, your survival brain doesn't stop to ask intelligent questions like, "Is this the best choice for me?" or "Can I do this a different way?" It just does what it's designed to do: react. Stress comes in all shapes and sizes but your brain, for better or worse, only has one (big!) response.

That geometry test isn't a life-or-death situation, no matter how much it may feel like one at the time. So, a full stress response in reaction to everyday pressures is too much of what's supposed to be a good thing. The human stress response is designed as a short-term, big-time reaction to *infrequent* situations. The trouble is, today's world is often chaotic, fast paced, and pressured. Many teens (like the ones who took our survey for this book) are dealing with what feels to them like high-stress situations every day.

Teen brain +
Being human +
21st- century stressors =

"Why did I *do* that?"

Overreacting to nonvolcanic, non-tiger situations can lead to a variety of problems that increase your stress level. Too often, people under stress do, think, and say the oddest—and even the worst—possible things. For instance, instead of telling your dad that you'll be there after you finish your math homework, you might repeatedly ignore him when he calls you for dinner and get into a needless argument as a result. Or maybe you yell at your little sister when you're actually stressed about something that happened during soccer practice. She ends up crying, and you end up feeling bad and getting in trouble. You look back later and find yourself saying, "I don't know what I was thinking!"

A classic "Why did I do that?" situation is cheating on a test. Suppose you're taking a history final that you studied for all week. You're stressed as you sit there waiting for the exam to be handed out, and when it finally lands on your desk, you look at the first question and go blank. You tell yourself that you don't know the answer—that, in fact, you don't even understand the question! In a blinding flash, everything you studied (dates, names, facts) vanishes. Even your ability to use a pencil seems to have disappeared. You start panicking because your grade depends on this final.

In desperation, you might peek at your friend's exam and copy an answer or two (or three), which you'd normally never do. Your stress response has just created a much bigger problem than brain freeze, because cheating can lead to major consequences. You survived, but you didn't think. And later, you're left asking yourself *why* you did what you did.

You can't shut off your stress response—it's millions of years in the making, and your survival brain isn't going to give up that easily. But you *can* learn to manage your stress more effectively. If you want life to be more than a repeating cycle of fight, flight, freak out, or freeze, you can learn to recognize your individual stress response and what triggers it. For now, just knowing about the three parts of the brain is a start. But you've also got to know a little something about yourself . . .

Who you are and what you think

How you deal with stress has a lot to do with the *temperament* you were born with and the thoughts and beliefs that you've developed over time. Your temperament affects how quickly you react to experiences and the intensity of those reactions. In other words, your temperament is a major player in how you respond to stress, and it can help you or get in your way.

If you had to pick ten words from the list on the next page, which ones would most accurately describe you? Put them together for a glimpse of your own fascinating temperament.

No temperament trait is necessarily "better" or "worse" than another, but it's undeniable that some traits are viewed more negatively than others. Remember that old rhyme "Sticks and stones may break my bones, but words can never hurt me"? That's not always true. The words you use to describe people (and yourself) have real power and can influence your perceptions of yourself and others.

Suppose you're going to meet someone for the first time, and you hear him described as "curious." Now suppose he asks you lots of questions and seems interested in your personal life—that probably fits with your expectations. But what if before you met this

What words describe you?

Accommodating	Fair	Persuasive
Active	Flexible	Pessimistic
Adventurous	Focused	Powerful
Affectionate	Forceful	Precise
Agreeable	Forgiving	Pushy
Blunt	Friendly	Quiet
Bold	Funny	Relaxed
Brooding	Generous	Reserved
Calm	Goofy	Resilient
Careful	Happy	Sarcastic
Cautious	Helpful	Sassy
Challenging	Imaginative	Self-assured
Compassionate	Impulsive	Sensitive
Competitive	Independent	Serious
Confrontational	Inquisitive	Shallow
Controlling	Kind	Shy
Cooperative	Lazy	Silly
Curious	Likeable	Steady
Cynical	Logical	Stubborn
Daring	Messy	Supportive
Decisive	Mixed up	Sympathetic
Deep	Neat	Tenacious
Determined	Nice	Timid
Diplomatic	Nonconfrontational	Thorough
Direct	Nosy	Thoughtful
Disciplined	Observant	Tolerant
Distracted	Open	Trusting
Easygoing	Opinionated	Trustworthy
Efficient	Optimistic	Unassuming
Emotional	Orderly	Unconventional
Empathetic	Outgoing	Watchful
Energetic	Patient	Weird
Excitable	Peaceful	Willful

guy someone described him as "nosy"? Your first impression of him could be quite different as a result and, possibly, his questions might annoy you. See the difference?

How you think of and describe yourself is as powerful as how you describe others. Do you think of yourself as "shy" instead of "cautious"? Do you say you're "weird," or do you call yourself "unconventional"? Wouldn't you rather be "tenacious" or "determined" than "stubborn"?

WRITE ABOUT IT: What are your strengths? What would you like to improve? Take the opportunity to be honest. Don't beat up on yourself or worry if you sound like you're boasting. No one has to look at the list but you.

Although you were born with your temperament in place, it isn't carved in stone. You can make certain kinds of changes. So, if you wish you could respond differently to stressful situations, know that it's possible. How you *feel* inside may not change, but what you *do about how you feel* can change. (Chapter 4 is filled with strategies you can try for reducing stress and handling situations more effectively.)

Your temperament is the starting point—but, over the years, you've developed a way of thinking, a belief system, and opinions about the people, places, and things you've come in contact with. Every experience you have helps shape who you become. Your family, friends, and community (in other words, your environment) all play a role too.

Here's an example of how this works: Perhaps you were at the beach for the first time as a young child, and you got knocked over by a wave. You churned around underwater until two strong hands pulled you to safety. You might have found the experience terrifying, or you might have found it exciting. You could come away feeling

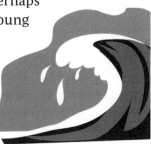

that the ocean is dangerous, you can't protect yourself, and you don't like the beach. Or you could see it differently—that water is exhilarating, your grandfather is a hero, and you want to learn how to swim. How might these opposing outlooks affect you in the future? Fast forward to ten years later: Your friends invite you to the beach and you're (1) too scared to go so you make an excuse, or (2) the first one in the water when you get there.

> **THINK ABOUT IT:** Is your head filled with statements like, "I'll never get this right," "I'm stupid," "I can't do it, so why bother?" "Everything's my fault!" or "My life stinks"? Or are you more likely to tell yourself, "I'm going to try my best" or "I know I can handle this"? Where do those thoughts come from? What beliefs are they based on? How do they affect your stress level?

Beliefs, no matter how they're formed, are powerful. They can open you to new experiences, or they can give you a laundry list of things to stress about. Fortunately, beliefs can be changed—much more easily than temperament. You can replace old ways of thinking, negative opinions, bad habits, and past patterns of behavior. Remember: Your brain is changing. It's adaptable!

* * *

In many ways, your brain is the home of everything that makes you *you:*

- your temperament
- your beliefs and opinions
- your feelings
- and last, but never least, your stress response

Understanding what's going on in your head—whether it's how your brain works or how your temperament leads you to react the way you do—can help you get a grip on stress. The more you know, the easier it will be for you to recognize what stresses you out and why—and that's half the battle right there. Next, you've got to know what your *body* has to do with it (Chapter 3 can help).

dating   jobs   family   pressure
cliques   homework   identity   tests
bullying   friends

3

Stress and Your Body

When **GRACIE** auditioned for the school musical, the competition was intense, but right after she'd finished, the director smiled at her and nodded. Gracie felt pretty confident that she'd gotten the lead—until a few days later when she walked into the chorus room to check out the cast list. A crowd was pressed in front of the bulletin board where the list had been posted, and Gracie's heart began to pound. "What if I don't get the part?" she thought. Her throat seemed to close up. She suddenly felt cold and shivery all over.

Gracie's stomach was tied in knots as she made her way through the crowd. She looked at the list to see whose name was next to the lead role. "I didn't get it," she realized. She frantically searched the rest of the list, trying to find her name. There it was, under "Chorus." Nearby, some of the students were so happy that they yelled and jumped up and down. But, in her disappointment, Gracie barely heard them. She felt like she was underwater and couldn't breathe. All she could think was, "I've got to get out of here."

Upset stomach. Pounding heart. Dry mouth. Shivers. A feeling of being unable to breathe. Signs of a terrible illness? No—just your average stress response. You've probably felt it before.

Here's a breakdown of what can happen from head to toe when you're under stress:

30

- Your face may heat up, and your cheeks or ears may redden (signs of ramped-up blood circulation).

- Your pupils dilate to improve your vision.

- Your breathing automatically shifts to your upper chest and becomes more rapid and shallow (in fact, you may feel as if you can't quite catch your breath). You start breathing faster because your body needs to quickly increase the amount of oxygen being circulated in your bloodstream.

- Your heart rate increases (that explains the pounding). Because your body needs oxygen-rich blood to flow to your leg and arm muscles, your heart starts to work harder in anticipation of running or fighting.

- A surge of stress hormones, such as *adrenaline* and *cortisol,* flow into your bloodstream, giving you extra energy, strength, speed, and endurance. These hormones instantly put you on alert.

- Your digestive system shuts down so that energy can travel to where your body most needs it. You may quickly lose your appetite and get a dry mouth. If your breakfast or lunch is still being digested, the acids slosh around in your stomach because digestion's been interrupted. Your stomach may feel like it's churning.

- You begin to sweat, and your hands and feet may get cold and clammy. That's your body's cooling system turning on to counterbalance all that heat you're generating from the extra energy you produce.

> ## FACT!
> *When your stress response is triggered, two major body systems are called into action: circulatory (heart) and respiratory (lungs). Your digestive, immune, and reproductive systems shut down so their energy supplies can be used where you really need extra energy. Energy supplies aren't infinite. Over time, if your body's reserves are exhausted, you can burn out. You may not only feel fried but also get sick more frequently and have a harder time fighting off illnesses or recovering.*

Maybe you recognize some of these symptoms from your own experiences of pressure or big-time expectations. Who hasn't had sweaty palms and trouble breathing (or talking coherently) when a crush walks up, smiles, and says hi? Who's never felt like puking before taking a final exam or giving a speech? We've all been there, and it's no fun. Fortunately, those uncomfortable feelings usually don't last very long. Within a short time, the body's central nervous system calms down and returns to its normal state.

Q&A

How do you feel physically when you're stressed?

"I get either a headache or an upset stomach."
—Gretchen, 14

"I feel like I'm trapped in a cage."
—Colby, 12

"I feel like I just have to lie down and think about something else."
—Andi, 12

"I feel exhausted."
—Michale, 12

"I feel nervous and antsy."
—Paul, 13

"I feel fat, and I sleep."
—Jered, 13

"I feel like adrenaline is pumping through my veins really fast."
—Dan, 14

"I feel chest pains or get headaches if my stress is severe."
—Phil, 16

"It drains me physically. I feel tired yet can't sleep."
—Zoe, 17

"I don't feel like eating, even though that would normally be a time when I'm hungry."
—Walt, 18

"I feel worn out, like if I take one more step, I'll fall over and not move."
—Sasha, 16

So, what's the story behind all those physical reactions? To understand the effects of stress, try imagining your body as a car. (Go ahead and picture your ultimate car—any kind is fine, as long as it runs on gas.) Now think of your stress hormones as super-charged fuel boosters that are automatically added to your gas tank. The fuel boosters can hugely improve your car's performance in a short race. But suppose you're running at full speed and relying on boosters almost all the time? In the long run, boosters can really mess up the way the car responds, damaging the engine and how well it runs.

Short-term stress is like a little jolt to your system to help you succeed under pressure—a reminder that you're feeling temporarily off-balance and you need to take care of yourself. But long-term stress is another story. When your body is on high alert for extended periods of time, this takes a major toll on your body and mind.

The wear and tear of long-term stress

Long-term means "over a long period of time," but it's not always something that can be measured precisely in hours, days, weeks, or years. Think of a long-term stressor as any ongoing situation that feels pressured, tense, or out of whack in some way—and you don't know when (or if) it's going to end. Have you ever been in a rocky relationship, one that's filled with lies and disappointments? Or have you ever had a rough year in school? Over the long haul, the stress you experience from constant pressures like these can contribute to serious health problems. How serious? That depends on a few factors that are completely unique to you.

Three Factors

1. First, **genetics** (the genes you've been handed down from your parents) play a role because they factor into your physical makeup and your health. Depending on what you've inherited gene-wise, you may be more (or less) likely to get certain diseases or health conditions that long-term stress can contribute to.

2. Then there's your **temperament:** You may be the type of person who gets stressed easily and frequently, or you may be more laid back. How you handle your stress can help or hurt.

3. Last, you've got other **people in your life** who affect your stress level. If the adults in your family handle pressure well, that makes it easier for you because you've probably learned positive behaviors and attitudes from them. On the other hand, if your adult role models are unable to manage their stress, you may have learned some behaviors that make it difficult for you to get back in balance.

TALK ABOUT IT: You've got three factors to consider: your physical makeup, your temperament, and your stress-management role models. What do you know about all three? Talk to your mom or dad about your family's health history (both sides, if possible). Are there any relatives with high blood pressure or stomach problems? Any older relatives who have enjoyed a long history of good health? If you don't know your family's history, see a doctor to get information about your health and how you can take good care of yourself now and in the future.

THINK ABOUT IT: When it comes to stress management, who's your best adult role model and why? What can you do to follow in that person's footsteps?

WRITE ABOUT IT: In your journal, write down what you've learned about your family's health history, your own health, how you typically handle your feelings, and how the people around you handle theirs. Look at what you've written: Are the three factors working in your favor or not? What's helping? What isn't?

Long-term stress can really wear you down physically, but does that mean there's nothing you can do about it—that your destiny is set? No way! You've got choices about your body, how you handle your feelings, and who you look up to and reach out to. When you make positive choices, they can make a *huge* difference in your life. In fact, good choices help you reduce your stress level and lead a life that's healthier, saner, more balanced—and believe it or not, more fun.

Just remember that your #1 job, always, is to respect your body and everything that makes you who you are—in other words, take good care of yourself and get yourself back in balance.

What is your body telling you?

Your body is incredibly sensitive to changes. It often senses that a situation is stressful before you've even had a chance to recognize and identify the source. These body changes are an early warning system—nature's way of helping you survive. If you get into the habit of paying attention to them, you can get back in balance faster, and that's going to help you enjoy life more. So, what are *your* short-term stress symptoms? Do you get:

- a dry mouth?
- a flushed face?
- a rapid heartbeat?

- sweaty palms?
- cold hands and feet?
- a stomachache?
- all of the above?

These typical stress symptoms can be embarrassing, inconvenient, and/or uncomfortable, but they serve a purpose. They're your body's way of sending you messages about what you need to do to protect yourself and stay healthy. Are you paying attention to those messages? Just because you're not paying attention doesn't mean that your body is going to forget about the stress.

TAKE IT INTO THE REAL WORLD: Turn a magnifying glass on your stress response, as if you were a detective looking for clues to a mystery. How do you feel? How does your behavior change? Observe the people you live with by looking at the choices they make as a result of stress. Notice any patterns?

How do you know if you're dealing with *long-term* stress? In addition to the common symptoms of stress, you may also experience:

- frequent headaches
- frequent colds, sore throats, and/or pinkeye
- cuts or sores that seem to take forever to heal
- a tendency to overeat
- frequent loss of appetite
- trouble sleeping
- low energy levels

If you have several of these symptoms, long-term stress might be the cause. If that's the case, it's a good thing to know because what's stressing you out may not go away by itself. Now for the bad news: Unmanaged long-term stress can eventually lead to stomach ulcers, reproductive dysfunction (including low fertility), high blood pressure, or heart disease much later in life. But you *can* protect yourself. First, you may need some help identifying the source of your stress and dealing with it. You deserve that support, and you can find it. Take a look at Chapter 10 for some tips on getting professional help. In the meantime, you can check out the tools in this chapter for help in bringing more balance to your life.

TAKE IT INTO THE REAL WORLD: Pay attention not only to your stress symptoms but also to what triggered them. The goal here is to think about what's bothering you *as soon as you start to feel off-balance.* Next time you get those familiar feelings (upset stomach, breaking into a cold sweat), stop and look at the source. Decide what you can do that moment to take care of yourself.

Body balance—how to get it

You've got lots of choices when it comes to the way you respond to stress. Some choices can be used as emergency "first aid" measures to help you curb a stress response. Others can be thoughtfully considered and developed over time. When incorporated into your life, these stress busters help you maintain your balance, day after day. You'll find lots more tools in Chapter 4, but for now, check out the three basics of keeping your body in balance: *good nutrition, exercise,* and *sleep.*

Eat well, stress less

Your body needs energy to keep you alive from moment to moment. That energy comes from food. When you're stressed, your energy is depleted much faster than usual. (Remember, your brain thinks you're dealing with an emergency, and that gets your heart working overtime.) You may be extra hungry. Hunger will increase your stress, so you're going to want to eat something to help get your body back in balance. What you eat is always important. Your daily choice of food affects:

- how healthy you are now
- how healthy you'll be in the years ahead
- how you feel
- how you look
- how you manage stress

When you're off-balance, your body uses up certain nutrients quickly, including B vitamins—the ones your body needs to release energy and maintain a healthy nervous system. Good sources of B vitamins include fruits and vegetables, lean meats, and poultry. Eat these foods often to stay energized. To further maintain your energy level, eat small, frequent meals that contain complex carbohydrates like brown rice, whole grain bread, or whole grain pastas. These foods are digested slowly and supply a steady stream of energy to your body. (Tip: White rice and white bread *don't* have these same benefits.) Some experts also say that complex carbohydrates soothe your brain.

Limit the junk food like chips, doughnuts, fast food, ice cream, shakes, and cookies. It's easy to grab those foods when you're stressed and on the go, but they don't help your body feel better or stay healthy. And you might end up developing a habit of reaching for junk food each time you get stressed.

FACT!

Stressed? Eat a banana. Bananas are high in potassium, which is a mineral that helps send oxygen to your brain and normalizes your heartbeat—two helpful things when you're stressed.

Sugar: How Sweet Is It?

Sugar seems to be the ingredient of choice for most kids and teens (not to mention adults). It's the main ingredient in candy, sweets, and sugar-coated breakfast cereals, and it's the #2 ingredient in soft drinks. But what you may not know is that sugar is hidden in tons of other foods—everything from ketchup to bread. So, you're probably consuming even more sugar than you realize.

Because sugar is rapidly absorbed by the body, you might get a quick lift after you eat it. But the energy or feeling of comfort that you experience doesn't last long. A sugar buzz is usually followed by a sugar crash (leaving you tired and even more off-balance than before). What happens next? A sugar craving. Talk about stressful! Just keep this in mind whenever you're tempted to gulp down a couple of sodas or candy bars. Reach for some fresh fruit or carrot sticks instead.

Stress also speeds up how quickly your body uses water. Drinking some water is a fast and easy way to get your hydration levels back in check. But by the time you actually feel thirsty, you're already dehydrated. Studies show that you should drink at least eight glasses of water each day, not including other beverages made with water, like coffee, juice, or tea.

Lots of people skip water in favor of caffeinated drinks like coffee, sodas, or tea. Caffeine is a natural substance found in several plants (coffee beans, cocoa beans, tea leaves). But just because

FACT!

Dehydration can temporarily shrink your brain just a little. If you're stressed and already having trouble thinking clearly, you're going to need as much brainpower as possible. Try a glass of water.

caffeine is "natural" doesn't mean it's helpful, especially when you're stressed.

How often do you consume colas, chocolate, lattes, and frozen coffee drinks (all of which contain caffeine)? Some teens eat or drink this stuff all day long. Caffeine increases your level of the stress hormone cortisol (that's why you feel temporarily more alert after consuming caffeine). But whenever you ingest caffeine, you're actually *increasing* your stress. As with sugar, you may get a short-lived buzz—but you're in for a crash later. Caffeine consumption can become a major habit because of this up-and-down cycle. Your best bet? Cut out caffeine or at least reduce it. Breaking the caffeine habit isn't easy, but it's worth it—you'll feel calmer, less rushed, less jittery, and definitely more relaxed.

As for the rest of your overall healthy "body balancing" diet, a lot depends on your physical makeup, including your current age, your weight, and any special nutritional needs or restrictions (for example, if you're a vegetarian or you have food allergies or a medical condition). Talk to a knowledgeable adult about how to make sure your diet is not only healthy but right for *you.* You can see a doctor for this information or go to the school nurse. Parents and teachers can be good resources too.

To learn more on your own, check out the Harvard School of Public Health: Food Pyramids site (www.hsph.harvard.edu/nutritionsource/pyramids.html). You'll find comparisons of the U.S. Department of Agriculture's Food Guide Pyramid and Harvard's own Healthy Eating Pyramid. You can also go to Nutrition.gov at www.nutrition.gov to download a free copy of a brochure called "Finding Your Way to a Healthier You," based on the USDA Dietary Guidelines for Americans.

 TAKE IT INTO THE REAL WORLD: Because most of us normally eat too fast (and even more so when we're stressed), here's a "get-back-in-balance" activity for you. The next time you eat a snack or a meal, try to savor the experience. Pay attention to the food's color, size, aroma, temperature, and texture. Chew and swallow s-l-o-w-l-y. Stay in the here and now and try not to think about anything else but what you're eating and how much you enjoy it. How does this kind of experience differ from the way you usually eat?

Energize with exercise

Exercise and fresh air are good for you. You've probably heard this a million times, and it's true. But did you know that exercise is a fantastic stress buster? If you're worried about tonight's homework or the argument you had with your best friend, there's something you can do right now to get yourself back in balance: You can go outside for a walk or a run. It will leave you energized and clear your head in no time.

If the weather's bad or it's really late (or if you can't go out for whatever reason), you can still get the benefits of exercise. You don't need any special equipment or a lot of room to run in place or do push-ups, sit-ups, or jumping jacks. If you hate walking and running and you're not a fan of repetitive exercises, then get up and dance. You pick the music and make up the moves. It doesn't matter what you do—just do something active. Getting your body moving will help center you, physically and mentally.

If you make exercise a regular part of your day, your life will change for the better. Research shows that people who exercise regularly are not only healthier but also have lower stress levels and a more positive outlook on life (all good things that you deserve). Experts say that exercise helps release *endorphins,* which are like natural "feel good" chemicals in your body. Physical activity also boosts your self-esteem.

You may be thinking, "Regular exercise!? How can I add one more thing to my schedule?" Maybe an attitude shift will help. Instead of thinking of exercise as something you *have* to do or *should* do, think of it as a gift to yourself—something that you *get* to do.

The key to making exercise a regular part of your life isn't really about finding the time, it's about finding an activity you like so much that you want to stick with it (or about having lots of physical activities that you absolutely love). When you focus on fitness, you take care of yourself, build your endurance, and get stronger, faster, and more flexible. So, join a sports team, make the most of P.E. class at school, go for long bike rides on the weekend, get as much fresh air as you can, and see if you or your family can get a membership to a local gym. Walk, jog, dance, skate, or do whatever gets you moving—not just once a day but for short periods of time throughout the day. You'll feel better if you do.

Every time you take care of yourself by exercising, you're making a deposit into your stress-proofing bank account. The next time you're under pressure, you may find that you're actually less stressed than usual or that you can get yourself back in balance more quickly. It's definitely a goal worth working toward.

Gotta get some sleep!

Nobody knows *exactly* what sleep does for the body, but we do know that everyone needs it. In fact, your body and brain need sleep as much as food, air, and water.

People once thought sleep was downtime for the body and the brain. Actually, a lot of major chemical and electrical activity goes on while you sleep, and that's essential for your physical and mental health. For example, you're growing like crazy (especially between the ages of 13 and 16). Growth hormones are released at night, affecting your bones and muscles, your organs, and your brain development. Sleep is also important because it helps your body stay calmer and more balanced.

When you were younger, you probably went to bed early and got up early. Now your inner clock has shifted, which may make you want to go to sleep later and get up later. If life actually allowed you to do that, you'd be getting the sleep your body needs. Unfortunately, school demands that you get up much earlier than you'd like. You're probably still going to bed late and therefore not getting enough sleep. And sleep deprivation, like hunger or thirst, is a physical stressor. No wonder a lot of teens feel irritable and have trouble concentrating.

Sleep loss builds up. If you go without the sleep you need for too long, you weaken your body's ability to fight disease and repair injuries. So, what can you do? Try to get into some better sleep habits. Start going to bed at a regular time every night, so your routine becomes more predictable, and make sure this bedtime allows for *at least* eight hours of sleep. Here are some other healthy habits:

FACT!

You need about nine and a half hours of sleep each night. But only 15 percent of teens get that. Most only sleep between six and seven hours per night during the school week. And 23 percent of high school students say they fall asleep in class at least once a week.

- Avoid caffeine in the late afternoon or evening—it will keep you awake.

- Get as comfortable as possible every night. If your bed is a jumble of dirty sheets and homework papers, take a few minutes to straighten it up.

- Don't fall asleep in your clothes.

- Crack a window for some fresh air. Pull down the shades if you like a darkened room; you'll feel more comfortable and ready to relax.

- Do all those things you know you're supposed to do but sometimes feel too tired to bother with: brush your teeth, floss, wash your face, and so on.

FACT!

You can actually learn while you sleep. Experts say that you're much more likely to do better on a test if you get a good night's sleep than if you stay up all night cramming. Sleep actually enhances learning and memory because sleep makes the neural connections in your brain more elastic.

If you've had a late night and you're tired when you come home from school, take a quick nap (about 20 minutes). It will help you re-energize and feel more rested. Give yourself permission to take it easy: You're not a machine! If you allow yourself to relax and do nothing for a while, your body can recharge and your stress level will go down. Do you tell yourself that resting is a "waste of time"? Rest is as important to your body as bathroom breaks or meals. You'll work better and feel better after you've rested—so give yourself a break.

FACT!

If you're stressing over a problem right before you go to bed, you may be in for a sleepless night. But if you realize there's nothing you can do about it right now and consciously choose to wait until morning to think about it, you'll sleep a lot better. Zzzzzzzzzz.

One last thing to think about: Is it possible that you're getting too much of a good thing? A good night's sleep is healthy, but too much sleep can make you more tired or be a sign of underlying problems. If you're sleeping as much as 12 hours or so per night, if you take frequent naps, or if you constantly feel tired, these could be signs of depression, long-term stress, or a medical problem. Go see a doctor to get yourself checked out.

TAKE IT INTO THE REAL WORLD. Ever tried any yoga poses? They're designed to help your body relax. Here's a good one (and it doesn't involve wrapping your ankles around your neck). You'll need a big pillow, a folded towel, and a quiet place to lie down (the floor or a bed). Now follow these simple steps:

1. Lie on your back and bend your knees. Keep the soles of your feet flat.

2. Place the pillow under your knees for support and put the folded towel under your head.

3. Rest your arms at your sides; the palms of your hands should face up.

4. Close your eyes.

5. Relax your legs by taking some deep breaths and thinking, "Relax."

6. Now relax your belly. Keep breathing.

7. Relax your arms and your fingers. Feel your stress begin to drain away.

8. Relax your shoulders, neck, and face (your mouth, your eyes).

9. When you feel completely relaxed, take a few extra minutes to breathe slowly and calmly, and enjoy your rest.

10. Repeat whenever you'd like.

* * *

Now you know the basics: *Rest is calming and restorative. Exercise should feel good and be fun. Good nutrition fuels your body to help you stay healthy and less stressed.* Make these habits your own—practice them every day, if possible. You'll be keeping your body in balance in the short-term and keeping yourself healthy for life.

4

Your Stress-Busting Tools

Whether it's long-term or short-term, stress is still *stress*—and that means your thinking brain shuts down. It's no wonder that lots of teens say they feel "too stressed to think." The good news is that you can learn to tap back into your thinking brain during pressure-filled moments. It's kind of like outsmarting your stress. To do this, you need some tools to help you get through tough situations and make good choices (you'll find the tools starting on page 53). But you've also got to keep an eye out for the stress traps.

Stress traps (and how to break free)

Anyone can fall into a stress trap. Some people get caught in more than one. Others are so deeply trapped that they've almost forgotten there are better ways of coping. But there's one thing that's true for all of us: Being in a stress trap makes getting back in balance even more challenging (but still possible).

The stress trap lineup includes:

■ Avoidance
■ Procrastination
■ Obsessions
■ Worries

Avoidance

At lunch on the first day at her new middle school, **CARMEN** sat alone in the cafeteria. She wanted to join some of the students she'd met in math, but she couldn't get up the courage to go over to their table. While eating, Carmen noticed some other girls looking at her and laughing. She overheard one of them saying "Gorilla" and "Unibrow." It was obvious the girls were talking about her.

Carmen couldn't believe how mean they were being. "Should I say something?" she wondered. Instead of speaking up for herself, Carmen threw away her half-eaten lunch and went to her locker. Then she decided she'd go to the main office and call her dad, saying she was sick and needed to go home.

Before long, Carmen started getting stomachaches—real ones—every morning before school. She didn't have anyone to talk to in class. Everyone else seemed to have friends, and Carmen felt alone. She tried to be invisible and to pretend she didn't care what other people thought of her. And every day, she ate her lunch alone in the art room, where no one would notice her.

When the pressure is on, you might naturally feel the need to retreat to safety (also known as the "flight" part of the fight-or-flight response). But what happens if running and hiding is your main coping strategy? Well, you can become trapped.

If you avoid people or situations instead of facing them, your stress builds. You may start to cut yourself off from the world—and that makes it a lot harder to handle the pressures of daily life. Soon, you might find yourself running from any situation that stresses you out. Avoiding your problems won't make them disappear—they'll still be there, most likely growing bigger the longer you avoid them.

People have all sorts of ways of avoiding what's bothering them. Do any of the following ring a bell for you?

- You spend hours visiting chat rooms, surfing the Internet, playing video/computer games, or watching TV.
- You're alone a lot, even when you're at school. And after school, you don't do much with other people.
- You avoid talking to anyone about your problems because you don't want to face them, or you think other people won't care.
- You don't speak up when people hurt or anger you. Instead, you keep your feelings and frustrations inside.

 WRITE ABOUT IT: In your journal, start keeping notes about any possible avoidance activities. Pay attention to how much time you spend in front of the TV or computer; write the minutes or hours down afterward. Also, take a look at your social activities—do you have enough of them? Barely any at all? Too many? (Sometimes, teens avoid their stress by heading to the mall, going to a lot of parties, or spending almost every free minute with friends.) Ask yourself the most basic question: "Am I avoiding something—and if so, what is it?" Write your answer in your journal.

 THINK ABOUT IT: Can you recall a time when you kept quiet about something that was really bothering you? Did not talking about it make you more or less stressed? Why?

Procrastination

Two months ago, **TONY'S** English class was assigned a term paper. Tony started stressing right away because he hated the pressure of long-term assignments. He told his friend Alex, "There are all these steps you're supposed to do, like picking a topic and researching and doing footnotes. And then there's all the writing! It's too much!" Alex said, "It's a lot easier if you do a little every week so the deadline doesn't sneak up on you." Tony knew Alex was right and even made a schedule for himself to follow.

But here Tony was, a few days before his big deadline, without one word written, feeling completely freaked. He sat at his desk, staring into space. "There's no way I'll finish this," he told himself. He hadn't gotten much further than choosing his topic. He wondered if his mom could take him to the library, then realized it was closed this late in the evening. He knew his sister was using the computer for her homework, so there wasn't any way he'd get his research done online. He doodled a bit, thinking, "Okay, I'll start my paper in ten minutes." Ten minutes later, he started looking through some comics. Sighing, he turned on his CD player and listened to some tunes while lying in bed. "I'll get to my term paper by 10:30," he promised himself. It wasn't long before he was asleep.

That's called procrastinating . . . and it's a very sticky stress trap. When you put off doing stuff that you know you have to do, your workload piles up—and so does your stress. Pretty soon, you've got a lot of unfinished business, plus plenty of things that you never even started.

Look around: Are you surrounded by piles of dirty clothes and homework papers scattered everywhere? Do you have lists of tasks you were going to do but didn't? Or maybe you put off making a list, and now you're trying to keep it all in your head? Procrastination can make your days a lot more stressful, and that added pressure leads to more procrastination. Soon you're caught in a vicious circle.

Lots of people—even the smartest, most successful ones you know—tend to procrastinate. It's natural to put off the boring chores or the yucky ones (like cleaning the litter box). Who wouldn't prefer a day at the pool instead of staying indoors and crossing tasks off their to-do list?

There *are* times when doing something fun first can energize you to start one of those not-so-fun tasks you've been dreading. But just so you know, *postponing* something isn't the same thing as procrastinating. For example, you might decide to delay getting started on your homework so you can go out for a run first. That's a smart choice because getting some fresh air and exercise might give you more motivation. But if you make a bunch of excuses to avoid your homework ("I need to call some friends first," or "I'll get to my homework after my favorite shows"), you're procrastinating. Your homework won't go away—and your stress will build.

Maybe you tend to wait until the last minute to get big projects done, and you tell yourself that you "work better under pressure." Sure, waiting until your stress response kicks in can give you an adrenaline burst—but it doesn't mean you're *really* going to work better or more efficiently. It just means that you're working under the added burden of more stress.

TAKE IT INTO THE REAL WORLD: If you're currently putting off something you know you have to do, you probably feel anxious. Want to reduce that feeling right now? Go spend 15 minutes on that task. Suppose you need to reorganize your science notes. Set a timer and organize a few folders. When the timer goes off, you're done. Afterward, notice whether your attitude about yourself or the task has changed for the better. Do you feel a little relieved? More positive? Or ready to tackle the rest of your subjects? How's your stress level? Do you feel a bit more calm?

Obsessions

SHAY and **ALANA** met as sophomores and, for a whole year, they were boyfriend and girlfriend. Shay believed it was a perfect relationship—even their parents liked each other. But two months ago, Alana suddenly broke up with him and Shay hasn't felt normal since. He's tried talking to Alana about what happened, but she refuses to get into it. He thinks about her all the time. He can barely do his homework or study, and his grades have slipped. When he's not eating junk food or sleeping his weekends away, he's usually reading old emails from his ex.

Shay wants to move on, but he can't seem to get Alana off his mind. He watches her in school. He daydreams about their past. He even dreams of her at night. Shay's parents are worried about him. But he tells them, "I can handle it. Please just leave me alone." He doesn't like their interruptions. He'd rather think about Alana.

When you're obsessed with something, you think about it day and night. You can be obsessed with an idea (you believe your teeth are funny looking, so you're always covering your smile), with an activity (you can't stop playing video games), or with a person (every moment, you daydream about your crush).

Obsessions distract you from more important things, like your family, friends, and schoolwork. You may hit a point where losing yourself for hours almost feels like the norm. If you've reached this point already, then your obsessions are holding you back and limiting you from enjoying life to the fullest. Ask yourself if you feel "stuck," out of control, or powerless. If so, those are signs of being off-balance. But you still have *choices.* You can actively choose to make better use of your time. Keep reading for tools that can help.

THINK ABOUT IT: If you were Shay's friend, what advice would you give him to help him deal with his stress and his obsession with his old girlfriend? Have you ever felt your thoughts being pulled back to the same old place over and over? What have you done to get back in balance? How has that worked?

Worries

KIRK and his friends have been a tight group for a long time, but lately their relationship has changed. First, Brian got into drinking beer. Now all the rest of the guys are drinking on weekends too—except Kirk. They tell him getting drunk is fun and that if he tried it, he'd have a better time hanging out with them. His friends say that he cares too much about getting caught, becoming an alcoholic, or not being "good." But Kirk can't help being concerned about all that stuff. His dad has talked to him about his own alcoholism, and Kirk wants to play it safe.

These days, Kirk spends a lot of time worrying. He's worried that someday his friends are going to do something really stupid when they're drunk, like driving. He's worried they'll get in trouble if their parents find out about the drinking. He's worried he might lose his friends. He's even worried that he won't have anything in common with them anymore if he doesn't start drinking. On top of all that, he's worried about his grades in math and his batting average. Both his math teacher and the coach have talked to him about needing to improve. When his dad asks him what's going on, Kirk just says, "Nothing." He's worried his dad will be mad at Brian and the other guys. Kirk feels like nothing's going right anymore.

There *is* such a thing as a healthy worry. When Kirk feels anxious about his friends' drinking and the likelihood that they could get in trouble, those are healthy concerns. He cares about his friends, and he doesn't want to see them get hurt. And he's right to care about his grades and sports performance—two things that are important to him. But a lot of Kirk's worries fall into the category of unhealthy because they're so persistent and replay in his head constantly, making it hard for him to think about much else. They wear him down physically and emotionally too.

Even minor worries can throw you off-balance. And worrying a lot can launch you into orbit.

So, are you a worrier? Do you often think about all that could go wrong, even at times when your life is going well? Worrying is a sign of stress, but it's also something that worsens your stress over time. You'll feel tired and tense, drained of energy and positive thoughts. When you feel that way, it's even harder to break free from this stress trap.

This may come as a surprise, but at a certain point, continuous worrying becomes a *choice* you make. And that means you can choose *not* to worry. Instead, you can tell yourself that enough is enough, and that a better choice is to talk to someone about whatever's stressing you out. Talking about problems is a step toward solving them. And that can help you breathe a huge sigh of relief.

WRITE ABOUT IT: Pretend you're writing an email to Kirk. Give him some advice to help him stop worrying and to start solving some of the problems in his life. Or, if you prefer, write yourself some tips on replacing your worries with *positive* thoughts instead. For example, when thoughts like "I'm going to mess up" replay in your head, replace them with, "I'm going to give it my best shot." With practice, thinking good thoughts will come more naturally and some of your worries may fade.

The get-back-in-balance tool kit

Caught in a stress trap? Help is on the way! This section talks about four stress-relieving tools—*breathing, thinking, flexing,* and *choosing.* Anyone can learn to use these tools. It may take some time and practice for you to get comfortable with them. Keep at it, because there's a big payoff: You'll be less stressed and more in control of the choices you make in life.

Sometimes, you'll want to use all four tools (one after the other) to help you deal with a challenging situation. At other times, you may need just one or two tools to feel better. Here are two important goals for you:

#1 be aware of when you **need** the tools and

#2 know **how** to use each one

If you use the tools when you need them, they'll help you day-to-day in so many ways. You'll know how to regain your balance when you're stressed and how to make choices you feel good about.

One more thing before check-ing out your tool kit: Know that not every stressful situation in your life can be managed using a cou-ple of tools or a four-step process. Some stressors in life (like divorce, a death in the family, or being bul-lied) are too big to be dealt with on your own, even if you've got great

> **FACT!**
> *These tools work even better when you're taking care of the basics: eating right, exercising, and getting the sleep you need. (See Chapter 3 for more info.)*

tools. When facing big issues, talk to someone you trust. Keep tak-ing care of yourself in the meantime—but get some help.

Tool #1: breathing

Breathing is a powerful tool (yes, breathing!). It's so important that it should be the first thing you do whenever you need to get a grip. We're not talking about the kind of breathing you do all day and all night, without thinking about it. We mean a type of conscious breathing called a *re-centering breath*. When you're off-balance, getting back to your "center" always makes you feel better.

Here's how it works:

➥ Close your eyes and get as relaxed as you can.

➥ Close your mouth and inhale slowly through your nose. Your breathing should be slow and comfortable. If you have a stuffed-up nose, trying to breathe through it is going to be stressful, so don't. Try this breathing exercise another time, when you're feeling better.

➡ Make sure to take a deep breath. Shallow breaths only go as far as your chest. Breathe all the way down to your belly. You should feel your stomach rise as you inhale.

➡ Now just let your jaw drop open and exhale slowly through your mouth.

➡ Try it again: Inhale through your nose, and then exhale through your mouth.

➡ That's a re-centering breath.

➡ Slowly breathe in and out at least ten times. Repeat as often as you'd like.

THINK ABOUT IT: While you're still relaxed, ask yourself some questions. What did you notice during this breathing exercise—did anything change? What happened to your thoughts and/or worries? What happened to your stress level?

TAKE IT INTO THE REAL WORLD: Sometime between now and when you go to sleep tonight, there's a chance that you'll get stressed at least once. Instead of losing your cool, say to yourself, "I'm stressed." Then stop whatever you're doing and take some re-centering breaths. After you've calmed down, you'll be able to think about your next best move.

Why take re-centering breaths? It's about regaining your balance. When you give your brain and body a moment to calm down, your ability to think clearly improves. Breathing is something you can do whenever you need to. You could be in the middle of an argument, but if you just start to consciously breathe, you'll begin to calm down. You can take re-centering breaths in class, on the field, on the bus, at a party, wherever.

Breathing Really Works

When we talk with students at schools, we always demonstrate how to take re-centering breaths. Here's what some teens experienced when they tried it on their own:

"I was trying to study when my little sister came in and started to jump on my bed. I was ready to literally kick her out of the room when I remembered about re-centering. So I took six deep breaths and said, 'Hey, Katherine, I have a TON of work and I was wondering if you would go out for about ten minutes and let me finish.' My bed-jumping sister went out of the room, stopping to look at me for a second, and then scuttled away. For the first time ever, I had gotten my stress out of me by inhaling and exhaling. WOW!"
—Mandy, 12

"My mom and I were in the middle of one of our usual fights, and I was being rude. Then I stopped, confused, and thought, 'I need extra time alone to relax.' My mother had a very grumpy face, but then I took a couple of deep breaths and thought about what I'd done. Then I told her, 'I am so sorry, Mom, I didn't mean to yell at you, and I think we should have a little time-out and think about how we are both really stressed out.' So my mom actually left the room, and we were happy at dinner again!"
—Emma, 11

"I was taking a practice SAT. I realized that I was under stress when I had less than 15 minutes left for the section and still had many problems to complete. My heart was racing, and I was very nervous. When I breathed, I didn't notice much at first, but then gradually I began to relax. My head became clear, and I was able to think better (almost unnervingly relaxing, seeing as I am used to stress!). I am eager to try it during the actual SAT."
—Clive, 15

P.S. We'd like to know how re-centering breathing works for you. Send us a few sentences in an email and let us know what was going on before you took some re-centering breaths and what happened after: breathing@toostressedtothink.com. You may win a prize!

Tool #2: thinking

Once you've calmed down, you'll automatically start thinking more clearly. How does that happen? Remember how your survival brain hijacks your thinking brain the moment you start getting stressed? When you de-stress, your thinking brain climbs back into the driver's seat and helps you sort out your feelings, think about what you want, and consider all your options. You *need* your thinking brain so you can make choices you'll feel good about, instead of ones you'll later regret.

TAKE A BREAK AND BREAK IT DOWN

Before you can figure out what to do in a stressful situation, you have to ask yourself some questions: "What do I want? What would resolve this problem for me? How can I help make this happen?"

The answers to these questions may not be obvious right away. And with stress hormones still kicking around inside you, your first impulse might be to *react.* But if you jump too quickly, you won't give yourself time to weigh your options. That's why it's good to take a break if you can. Stop, think, and then think some more.

Of course, that's not always easy or possible. In some situations, you have to think and act fast—like when your teacher calls on you in class or when you're trying to make your point in a debate. But at other times, you *do* have the chance to look at your options. For example, say you're stressed out about your weekend plans; you promised your dad you'd hang out with Grandma, but then you heard about a party you don't want to miss. You're not sure what to do—but you know you'd rather go to the party than anything else. And maybe this is a sore spot for you because you feel like your dad expects you to have every weekend free for family stuff. So, do you blow up at him? Not if you breathe and weigh your options. You can probably work out a compromise, like spending Saturday afternoon with Grandma so you can go to the party that night.

In this case, the answers to the questions above might be: *I want to go to the party, see my friends, and have a good time. But I still want to visit Grandma because I don't want to let her down. I want to keep my promise to Dad too. It would help if Dad and Grandma could be flexible about when we get together. I might be able to ask for that flexibility. Maybe I could go to the party and see Grandma on the same day.*

KNOW YOUR OPTIONS

Different situations lend themselves to different solutions, but there are always four general options that can be used to improve just about any stressful situation:

1. *Speak up:* Take the direct approach whenever possible. Express your feelings appropriately and responsibly to the people who need to hear what you have to say. Even if they don't agree with you, you'll feel less stressed after you talk about what's going on.

2. *Talk to a friend:* Good friends can help by listening, being supportive, and giving you advice or another perspective. Just knowing that someone else understands what you're dealing with can be a great stress reducer.

3. *Get help from an adult:* In some situations, you may find that you need the help of caring, trusted adults. They can listen to what's bothering you, offer support, give you access to more resources, and possibly intervene on your behalf.

4. *Take time to reflect:* You always have the option of postponing your decision to act. Taking a break is a good choice, as long as you come back to the situation when you're ready to act. You may find it helpful to listen to soothing music and write in your journal while you're thinking about what to do.

As you weigh your options, remember that not everything is within your control. For example, you can't control the weather or the fact that your brother is better at math than you are. You especially can't control the choices other people make, how they feel, or what they think. But you *can* control how *you* respond. When you think about your goals and options, consider what's realistic and reasonable in your situation, and let that be your guide.

Tool #3: flexing

When you hear the word *flexing,* you probably think of bending and stretching (how you *flex* your body). The kind of flexing we're talking about here is an *internal* bending and stretching. Flexing in this sense is:

> a conscious choice to do something different from your usual way of responding under stress.

In Chapter 2, you learned ways that your temperament and beliefs can increase or decrease your stress level. Depending on what you discovered about yourself, you probably have one or two (maybe more) traits that you'd like to flex. For example, if you tend to be high energy and impulsive, and your stress reaction is to lash out at people, then you might want to figure out ways to stay cool during high-pressure moments. Or, if you've got an active imagination and a tendency to worry, you may be looking for ways to rein in your thoughts and calm down.

So much depends on who you are, and that's why knowing yourself is key to figuring out how to flex. If you haven't already read pages 25–29, you may want to do that now. What you learn about yourself can help you better understand how flexing can work to your advantage.

NATALIE normally felt stressed when it came to trying new things. Her parents often called her "reserved," and she always thought of herself that way as well, even though she didn't like that description. By the time she was in eighth grade, she was fed up with the nervousness she usually felt in new situations. She wanted to be more social and outgoing.

So, the summer before ninth grade, Natalie thought it over and made a conscious choice: "When I walk down the hall in my new high school, I'm going to quit looking at my feet. Instead, I'm going to look people in the eye." She decided that it was worth a try to appear more friendly and confident on the outside—and that, hopefully, she would start feeling that way inside too.

Natalie flexed, deciding to work on her inborn trait of shyness. To her amazement, it wasn't that difficult for her to do. During that first week of school, she made eye contact with a lot of people and tried to appear friendly. By the following week, she had consciously chosen to start smiling at people and saying hi. The payoff was immediate—most people smiled back. Soon Natalie had a new way of handling herself in unfamiliar social situations. She noticed that her stress level was lower and that her confidence was higher. Within the first month of school, she had two new friends.

Is flexing simply a matter of, "I want to change, so now I'm going to make it happen"? Partly. But changes don't occur overnight, and they certainly don't happen as if by magic. It takes work— sometimes *hard* work. But it can be done.

How to start? First, think about whether you're bogged down in one of the stress traps (pages 46–53). If you are, making a change in this area could be a great place to begin. Let's say you have a tendency to procrastinate when you're stressed, and you put off your chores, homework, and big assignments. Ask yourself what role your temperament and beliefs might play:

- Do you tend to feel overwhelmed when under pressure, which affects your energy level?

- Do you have trouble focusing, making it harder to stay on task?

- Are you a perfectionist, thinking your work has to be flawless (so you can't get started because the expectations on yourself are so high)?

- Do you forget to write stuff down or not know how to get organized? Are you easily distracted?

Maybe none of these descriptions fit you. Maybe you see yourself as having a combination of the traits and attitudes listed above. The point is to do some thinking about how your personality plays into your stress response—and what you might change for the better.

Once you've identified an area you'd like to work on, plan the steps you need to take. Some steps might include buying a day planner or notebook, which can help you keep a schedule, and making to-do lists each day so you know what tasks you plan to complete. Or, you might talk to a parent or teacher about what's going on and ask for tips on staying motivated. Maybe you need to give yourself small rewards for completing homework or chores. That's *flexing*— it's about changing the way you normally do things so you can minimize stress and boost your confidence.

 TAKE IT INTO THE REAL WORLD: Sometimes, flexing means changing the way you interact with people. Suppose you get grumpy when you're under stress, and you take out your feelings on your family members. They fire back with some not-so-kind words, and the situation escalates. How could flexing help? You might decide to switch gears by telling yourself you're *not* going to be grumpy. Take a few re-centering breaths or do a physical activity that helps lift your spirits. Approach people as if you're in a good mood. Ask questions or talk about your day. Find something that will make you laugh, like a comic strip or humorous Web site. Keep looking for other ways to flex—you might be surprised at how these little changes make a difference.

Here's another way flexing can work: The next time you're in an argument with someone, stop and ask yourself, "What (if anything) would I lose right now by changing my behavior? And what (if anything) would I *gain* right now by changing it?" Then flex and see what happens.

Tool #4: choosing

Life is filled with choices. Some are easy, while some aren't. But whether the choices you make are difficult or a snap, you want to try to make them *consciously* and *deliberately*. Basically, that means thinking before you act or speak, and making choices that are right for you.

Can you remember a time when you were in a stressful situation, and you did something (or nothing) and later regretted that choice?

"My entire junior year I overate because I was so stressed. I gained like 40 pounds!"
—Lynn, 17

"I hit a friend and didn't do anything about it. And I feel bad now."
—Raoul, 14

"I hung up on my friend when she didn't want to go to my birthday party. I thought she didn't want to go because of some people she didn't like. It turns out her dad fell and almost broke his back."
—Rachel, 12

"I had to pick sides, and I chose my boyfriend instead of my best friend. I regret that like crazy!"
—Maria, 14

"A friend of mine told an anti-Semitic joke to me and a couple of other people, and I was too shocked to tell her that the joke had hurt my feelings. I regretted not setting her straight later on because, after the incident, there never seemed a right time to bring it up again."
—Sam, 14

"A man was being teased on the bus by some boys, and I didn't help him. I still feel really bad."
—Wen, 15

"I went to a wedding this year, and after the reception, I decided to go home since I had a headache. Everyone else wanted to go clubbing. I could see that the people who were driving were already drunk, but I convinced myself they'd be okay and I left. Later, I was told that they'd been in an accident. I really regret not stopping them or offering to drive them myself since I hadn't been drinking."
—Dawn, 19

"When my mom had breast cancer, I didn't help her out at home and did nothing to make her feel better."
—Ashley, 19

Can you recount a time when you were under stress but made a positive choice?

"When my mom blamed me for something, I didn't yell at her. I didn't take it out on her."
—Angelique, 12

"A group of my friends began doing things I didn't agree with. I stopped hanging out with them."
—Theo, 13

"When my friend's parents were going through a divorce and it put a lot of stress on her (and me), I spent time with her and just listened to her talk about her feelings. In some ways, I feel that it helped her relieve her stress, and I think I did the right thing by being there for her at such a confusing time."
—Mathilde, 14

"When my friend offered me drugs, I said no and walked away."
—Jon, 16

"I said no to a guy about sex, even though I wanted him to like me. I felt stronger."
—Tamara, 17

"I stole a football jersey, but then I got so stressed over it that I just brought it back."
—Chen, 13

"One time, my dad made a comment I thought was quasi-racist, so I told him to stop and he did."
—Bryce, 13

"I stood up for friends of mine who were being bullied."
—Charlotte, 13

"I recently got into a fight with my friend. I remember him spreading harsh rumors and embarrassing me. I was stressed to the point where I needed emotional support. I asked my school counselor for help."
—Steve, 13

As a teen, you have more choices than you had back when you were just a kid. You've got more control over everything from what you eat to where you go on weekends to who you hang out with. Does that mean you have 100 percent control over every choice in your life? Probably not. The adults in your family have a say about your curfew, your responsibilities at home, what you do during the summer, and many other things. Still, you're old enough to speak up about what you want and need. And you've got a lot of power when it comes to making good choices in your life.

If you make positive choices, you'll find that your life is more balanced. You'll have better relationships with family members, friends, teachers, and boyfriends/girlfriends. Why do choices matter so much? Because they affect your health, your stress level, your outlook, and your peace of mind. Your choices also affect other people, for better or worse. If you make choices that hurt others, you can probably guess the results—you might have regrets, get in trouble, or damage your relationships. And who wants *that?*

CHOOSING IN THE MOMENT

Some decisions have to be made quickly, without allowing much time to think. For example, you might have to choose what to say to a friend who's teasing you. Do you tease your friend back? Walk away without a word? Tell your friend to shut up? Laugh? Say, "That's not cool, could you stop?" Which choice will lead to the best outcome? Check in with yourself quickly to see how you feel about each choice and the potential results.

Of course, this is harder when you're stressed. Use your other tools, like breathing, thinking, and flexing. Calm down first, then think about what you want and how to get it. What's worked well in the past? What might work best now? Then decide.

CHOOSING WHEN YOU'VE GOT TIME TO THINK

Some choices are big and have long-range implications. And that means taking some time to think about them. For example, suppose you're trying to figure out which summer job to choose—the one that pays more or the one you think will be the most fun? Or, maybe you're deciding whether to go to college or which college you might want to attend. Perhaps you're faced with a choice about getting more intimate with your boyfriend/girlfriend. You know these choices will have consequences—so how do you know what's right for you?

You don't have to make choices like these all alone. Is there an adult you can talk to? Someone you trust to listen to you and give you some advice? How about a friend or an older sibling or cousin? When you talk to other people, you get their perspectives and opinions, and that can help you shape your decision.

Another option is to write your thoughts in your journal. That's a place where you can be totally honest, without worrying about what anyone else might think. Spend some time writing about what you imagine some of the consequences might be and how you think you'd feel about them.

You might also want to make a list of pros and cons for each choice. Just take a sheet of paper and write down what you're trying to decide at the top, draw a line down the middle of the page, and write the word *Pros* in the first column and *Cons* in the second. Take some time to think about what's positive or negative about each possibility. If your list contains mostly pros, then that's a good sign. On the other hand, if you have a lot of cons, maybe that choice isn't right for you. Only you can decide.

THINK ABOUT IT: Think of your favorite book or movie. Now ask yourself about the main character: What critical choices did he or she have to make, and what were the consequences? What was difficult about making those choices? What might have happened had he or she chosen differently?

CHOICES YOU REGRET

Bad choices usually don't "just happen." Often, they're made when you're under stress, off-balance, and not thinking clearly. Many of us make unconscious choices (the ones we make without thinking) when we're stressed. Instead of thinking things through, we just react. Or we're on automatic pilot, and the next thing we know, we've done something that leaves us asking, "What just happened?! I can't believe I did that."

That said, not all unconscious choices are bad. Sometimes, they have little significance (you put on unmatched socks without noticing). At other times, an unconscious choice can work to your advantage (you weren't paying attention to where you were going, took a wrong turn, and ended up finding money on the sidewalk). On the other hand, many of the choices that are made without thinking can have negative, and lasting, results. You've probably made a few choices like those, just like the rest of us.

Mistakes happen. We all make them, and we've all had regrets. It's just not possible for human beings to do everything perfectly or to make the right choice every time. But we all have the amazing ability to learn from our mistakes. That's how we grow in positive ways.

Instead of punishing yourself for mistakes, ask yourself what you learned. Analyze what you'd do differently next time. Talk to someone about what happened, if you'd like. Most importantly, don't beat yourself up over mistakes. Forgive yourself and move on.

* * *

Your tool kit is there for you at all times—but you need to know *when* to use it and *how* to use it. That takes practice. Start now and see how the tools work for you. The more you get used to them, the more comfortable you'll feel putting them into action every day. Pretty soon, you might even wonder how you ever got along without them.

PART
2

Working Through the Conflicts

5

You and Your Family

Everyone's got a family of some kind, and the package usually includes a lot of great stuff, along with the not so great. On the plus side, your brothers and sisters (if you have them) can be your best friends and provide tremendous support. After all, there's no one who better understands what it's like to deal with your parents.* And speaking of parents, having their love and acceptance is a huge plus. The encouragement they offer can help you maintain your balance or regain it when life gets hectic.

Maybe you can recall a time you were stressed and a parent or another family member gave you a hug, some valuable advice, and/or a chance to talk about what was on your mind. How did that affect your stress level? Did you feel stronger, knowing that you had someone on your side? Most of us need our families to be our safety net and support system. They're the people we go to first when we want help or a shoulder to cry on—they're often the ones who know us best and care about us most. Your family *should* be your rock. When life makes you crazy, time with your family *ought to* help you re-center and get back in balance so you can make good choices. But "should" and "ought to" can be very different from "what is."

---

*In this chapter, we use the word *parent* (or *parents*) to indicate an adult you live with who takes care of you. You might not have two parents or even one. You may live with one or more stepparents, grandparents, foster parents, relatives, or guardians. No matter who's taking responsibility for guiding you through your first 18 years of life, that adult *is,* in a sense, your parent.

Not all families are perfect—far from it. Conflicts come with the territory, especially during the teen years. Maybe you and your mom fight a lot, or you can't seem to get along with your younger brother. Or, maybe your parents seem to have too many rules or too little trust in you. Perhaps you no longer feel as close to the adults in your family, now that you're growing older and figuring out who you are apart from them. If your family relationships are changing (as they no doubt are, since you're a teen), you may feel tense and confused at home. And that's *stressful.* Home is supposed to be the place where each of us feels a little more peaceful and safe.

So, what can you do to help make your home a place where you feel calm, balanced, and free to be who you are? Well, you can't change who your family is or how each person behaves—but you *can* change how you respond. You've got control over what *you* say and do. If you've been practicing the tools from Chapter 4 (breathing, thinking, flexing, choosing), then you're already on your way toward becoming a more balanced, clear-thinking person. You can teach your family to use those tools too, if they're open to learning. And you can focus on staying connected to your family through all the ups and downs, instead of pulling away.

This chapter includes ideas on dealing with conflict and learning to handle some of the tough situations many families go through. But remember, each family is unique. If your family's problems go a lot deeper than those described in this chapter, turn to Chapter 10 for help. You always have the choice to reach outside of your family for further support, if needed.

THINK ABOUT IT: It's a fact of life: Teenagers complain about their parents (and vice versa). But does negativity ever help? Nope. What about flexing to change this habit? Instead of focusing on what bugs you about your dad or mom, look at what you appreciate about him or her. Try to make changes in the way you think and talk about your parents. Start a conversation with a sibling about the positive things the adults in your family do. For example, how do they help you when you're stressed? Do they ever make you laugh? How do they show they care?

TAKE IT INTO THE REAL WORLD: Your parents weren't handed an instruction manual the day you came into their lives, so they learn as they go. Sometimes, parents need to hear when they're doing something right. Let the adults in your family know that you appreciate their efforts. Offer a compliment here and there like, "Thanks for listening, Dad, I feel a lot better." Take this further by doing something to make a parent's day less stressful. Without being asked, do some laundry, help a sibling, or prepare a meal. Your positive words and actions mean a lot. In return, the grown-ups in your family may be more likely to do something nice for *you*.

Family conflict

When it comes to shared experience, and often even biology and genes, no other people are as much like you as your family. But you might feel as if you couldn't possibly be more *different.* As a teen, you're gaining more independence. You're growing and changing physically and mentally every day, and all those changes can leave you feeling like you don't know who you are. Throw in other stressors like household rules, curfews, parental expectations, and what do you get? Probably a feeling that no one understands you or lets you be yourself. Talk about stressful!

What's *really* behind some of the tension, though? Take a closer look:

A clash of temperaments: Your inborn temperament guides your responses to people, events, and the world. Your temperament is totally unique—and surprisingly, it might be completely different from that of your parents or siblings. Suppose you're the quiet poet in the family, but your sister is into sports and everyone's always loudly supporting her games—that might get to you. Or, what if you're naturally outspoken, and others in your family tend to hold back? A clash of temperaments can make living together challenging. You and your family members may not always see eye to eye.

Differing opinions: Your parents may have helped shape who you are, but you're still very much your own person. You've got your own opinions and outlook on life. These days, your opinions might differ from those of the adults in your family. You may think you deserve more freedom to speak your mind and do your own thing. On the other hand, your mom or dad may believe that your opinions are out of line or that your attitude needs readjusting. These clashes of opinion can lead to . . . what else but more stress?

Stressors: Is there something that always sets you off at home? It could be anything: a word, a tone of voice, a certain "look." Those are your family related stressors—they heat you up and trigger a stress response. Many teens have a lot of hot-button issues in their lives, check out what some of them had to say.

Family Related Stressors

My dad telling me to get off the phone · My mom telling me to clean up my room · My sister bragging about how many guys like her · My little brother whining · My mom saying, "I need to talk to you" · My brother's smelly T-shirts · My grandfather saying, "In my day . . . " · The phone ringing really early in the morning · When people call me "Red" · My cat making a gross coughing noise · My dad singing Beatles' songs (or anything) · My parents bragging about how many points my brother scored in his last game · When my parents order me around · My parents' fighting · My sister saying, "Can you do me a favor?" · Nagging · My sister being really fresh and always getting in trouble · My stepmother's voice · My brother's weird laugh · Crying babies · When my mom says, "Can we talk about this later?" · When my father calls five minutes before he's supposed to pick me up, and he's late · When no one listens to me

Temperament. Opinions. Stressors. Any and all of these can be sources of family conflict. As the pressures build, everyone in the family (including you) senses the tension and starts to stress. When your stress response is triggered, it's natural to react instead of thinking clearly about what's going on. You might start snapping, yelling, and slamming doors. The people around you may do the same.

Not everything is within your control, including your stress response (read up on it in Chapters 2 and 3). You're also not in control of:

- who your parents and siblings are
- the choices they make (or have made in the past)
- their beliefs and attitudes
- the rules and the consequences for breaking them
- the fact that you're a teen and still dependent on the adults in your family

Trying to change these things is like trying to knock over a concrete wall using just your own strength. Push all you like, scream as loud as you can, but your stress level will keep rising, and the wall won't budge. Still, you *do* have the power to:

1. Use the four tools in your "get-back-in-balance tool kit." (See pages 53–66.) You can put the tools to work any time you're stressed, unbalanced, or upset. You can also share the tools with your family so they have help when they need it.

2. Learn about your temperament. (See pages 25–29.) The more you know yourself, the better you'll understand what makes you tick, what drives you crazy, and what you need to do to take care of yourself.

3. Know your own stressors. Look at the list on page 72 to see if you relate to any of those. Getting familiar with things that set you off means you won't be caught off guard by them. Breathe when you start to get stressed and tell yourself that you won't overreact.

4. Be aware of your family members' stressors. Does it drive your mom nuts when you leave lights on in every room? Does your brother get tense the moment you start talking about a certain topic? It's easy to push people's buttons, especially when you're stressed or angry. But that only leads to more fights and frustration.

5. Take a look at your beliefs and opinions. Are they working *for* you or *against* you? In other words, do they help make you a stronger person and improve your life and relationships? Or, are they somehow holding you back? How do you *express* those opinions? Do you share them respectfully? How do people usually respond? Be honest as you think about these questions. You may need to flex some of your personal beliefs and opinions—or at least how you express them—to get along better at home.

Yes, your parents and siblings can be a major challenge to your sanity, but any relationship is a two-way street. If you understand how arguments play out between you and your family and use what you know to change what you can control, then you'll start to get along better with everyone. And that's going to help you stress less.

Q & A

What stresses you out about your family?

"My parents are finalizing their divorce. What if they ask us who wants to stay with whom? I love both of them very much, and if I choose one of them, the other might feel (I don't know what)."
—Sofia, 14

"My aunt, uncle, and cousin have currently moved into our household and have been living here for almost three weeks. Our house is built with two rooms (with no doors), a bathroom, a kitchen, and a living room. My relatives are driving me insane."
—R.J., 15

"I had a disagreement with my parents over my grades. I got stressed out because we always have that conversation, and it never gets resolved."
—Creighton, 12

"My mom doesn't listen when I say she needs to trust me more."
—Zack, 14

"I have a little sister. She's only 8, but she bugs me to death. I feel like hitting her all the time, but then I would get in trouble."
—Alex, 13

"My parents are always nagging and fighting with each other. I really don't know what to do anymore, and I want to run away."
—Marita, 15

"Every time I go home, my brother is waiting there to yell and scream at me, or tell me everything that I've ever done wrong."
—Siobhan, 15

"My dad demands the utmost respect from me, yet he gives none back. What reason would I have to give him any then?"
—Len, 17

"All of my conversations with my mom end up in boring lectures that make me want to go to sleep. So, after about five minutes, I start to get bored and distracted, and she tells me I'm being rude."
—Ethan, 15

Fighting about the rules

It's the parents' job to set up rules to keep their children safe—and it can almost seem like it's a teen's job to question those rules. Maybe you think of the household rules as a sign that the adults in your family don't trust you, or they don't believe that you're as mature and responsible as you know you are. You may also resent the rules if they're stricter than the ones your friends have. Or, perhaps you're the kind of person who tends to rebel against any limits on your freedom. No matter what the situation might be, it's hard to see rules as a "positive." After all, even if they *are* there to protect you, the rules make it harder for you to be as independent as you want to be.

KAISA'S mom spent her childhood in another country, and she has strict ideas about what kinds of clothes are appropriate for her 15-year-old daughter. Kaisa's been told that she can't wear tank tops or mini skirts like all her friends do. Although Kaisa loves many of the traditions from her mother's homeland, she thinks the dress code that her mom enforces is humiliating. Almost every week, she and her mother have some argument about Kaisa's choice of clothes.

Today, Kaisa got up early and tried to sneak out of the house with bare legs under a skirt that hung a couple of inches above her knees. She knew the skirt looked great on her and that it was a lot more modest than what her friends might wear. To her surprise, her mom had risen early too, and was in the kitchen making breakfast. Her mother looked at her in disgust and exclaimed, "Take that skirt off right now and go change clothes. You cannot dress like that for school. Or anywhere!"

The next thing she knew, Kaisa found herself shouting at her mother so loud that everyone else in the house woke up. "It's not fair!" Kaisa yelled. "I'm not you! I'll never be you, and I don't want to be you! Why can't you just let me be ME?" She ran to her room and slammed the door behind her. She could feel her heart pounding and hear her mom's footsteps coming down the hall. In an instant, she regretted what she'd just done. She realized she'd only made her situation worse.

Like Kaisa, you may feel stressed and squeezed by the rules, especially if they seem harsh or unfair, or if they make you stand out from other people your age. What can you do? Breaking the rules isn't an option—it will probably get you in trouble. Fighting about the rules leads you nowhere. And while rebelling may get people's attention, it won't necessarily get you what you want. Is there any other choice?

You could try compromising. By calmly and respectfully working together, you and your parents just might reach an agreement that both sides can live with. Your parents may be willing to loosen up on one or two of the rules, if you agree to follow them without complaint and show you can be trusted. Once you prove yourself, your mom and dad may be more flexible about other rules as well. This isn't something that happens all in a day. You have to flex and keep giving a little to get some of what you want.

 WRITE ABOUT IT: Write your ideas for a compromise that might resolve some of the issues between Kaisa and her mom. Have you ever been in a similar situation? If so, what was the outcome? Knowing what you know now, what might you do differently next time?

 TALK ABOUT IT: Talk to the adults in your family to find out what rules they had to follow at your age. Did the rules seem fair or not? What were the consequences for breaking them? Was there anything positive about the rules, and if so, what?

 TAKE IT INTO THE REAL WORLD: An "all or nothing" attitude usually increases stress and prevents conflict resolution. The next time you're in a head-to-head conflict with a parent or sibling, flex. Instead of thinking you have to get your way or win at all costs, consider a compromise. Can each of you bend a little? What might this do for your stress level and for the relationship?

Broken trust

Sixteen-year-old **SYD** had been living with his older sister, Cara, who became his guardian after their dad died. For the most part, Syd and Cara got along well, and Syd tried to follow her rules. He cleaned up the apartment while Cara was at work, and he did his homework without being asked. Some nights, he'd get dinner started before Cara came home.

But last weekend, things changed. Cara had to put in some overtime, and Syd was bored and decided to invite a few friends over. Somehow, more people showed up than he expected, because some of his friends brought over their friends. A few of the girls smoked, and Syd didn't know how to tell them it wasn't cool with him. Instead he just kept quiet. When his friends raided the fridge, Syd was mad but he didn't tell them to stop. After everyone had finally left, the apartment smelled from cigarettes and dirty dishes littered every table and counter. Cara came home to the mess and felt like Syd had really let her down.

Have you ever broken a parent's trust? Or felt like you really let an adult in your family down? Have you made bad choices, and then heard from a parent that you "can't be trusted"? Most likely, you have at some point, and you know how stressful that can feel.

On the flip side, has an adult ever done something that affected *your* trust? Or let *you* down? We're all human, and we all make mistakes. Sometimes, our mistakes lead to a breach of trust, which can shift the balance of a relationship. What if, for example, you discovered a dark secret that a parent was trying to hide or you learned that an adult in your family had done something you consider wrong? That could throw you completely off-kilter. You might doubt that you could ever trust him or her again—or any other adults, for that matter. The foundation of your relationship would have been shaken.

In the story above, Syd learned a lesson about trust. His sister Cara wasn't sure she could trust Syd to have friends over anymore, unless she was in the apartment to supervise what went on. Syd realized that he had gotten used to his sister's trust—that he'd earned it—and that not having it anymore really hurt him. To make matters worse, he had trusted his friends to come over and not trash the place, and they'd let him down. Syd was so stressed that he didn't make the best choice at the time. But now, what might Syd's next move be? He could:

a. call his friends and yell at them.

b. tell Cara that if she won't trust him, then he doesn't care and he won't bother trying to be "good" anymore.

c. take off for a few days, because why should he have to put up with this stuff?

d. apologize to Cara, explaining that he didn't mean for the situation to get out of hand and he's learned something from the experience.

What would *you* do? What would you NOT do? Which choice might lead to the best outcome?

Here's what *could* happen:

a. If Syd calls his friends and yells at them, they'll probably get mad back, and that won't solve anything.

b. If Syd starts an argument with Cara, threatening to stop being "good," then, in a way, he's making what happened *her* fault. She'll probably trust him even less.

c. If he leaves, Syd is running from his problems instead of facing them. He won't make peace with his sister, and he could even put himself in danger.

d. By apologizing, Syd could repair any damage he's done to his relationship with Cara. Most likely, she'd forgive his mistake and tell him what he can do to earn back her trust.

Like everything in a healthy relationship, trust has to go both ways. You need to trust the adults in your family to be there for you, and they want (and need) to be able to trust you too. If trust isn't at the core, then the relationship is unbalanced and may become a major stressor in your life. You can work on rebuilding trust by doing some of the basics: keeping your word, being honest, not making promises you can't keep, showing up when you say you will, and apologizing if you've hurt or angered someone, then making amends. Help the people in your family see that they need to do the same for *you.*

But maybe the problems in your home are more serious than what most families face each day. Perhaps you have difficulty believing that families are supposed to be supportive and loving because that hasn't been your experience, or perhaps you're not used to connecting with a parent or having one take care of you. Maybe the adults at home have substance abuse problems, are abusive to you or each other, are hardly ever around, or for one reason or another, neglect their roles as parents. If any of this is the case, then you may have had little reason to trust them or to believe they know what's in your best interest.

It's painful when the adults you should be able to count on aren't there for you. But don't give up on finding adults you can trust. Look outside of your family for supportive adults who can help you with your problems and guide you to make good choices. Reaching out to others is a stress reliever—more than that, it's a way to stay connected, safe, and strong.

To find caring, supportive adults, look to:

- adult relatives or older siblings/cousins
- adults at school, such as teachers, coaches, advisors, the school counselor, or your principal
- your best friend's parent
- adults at your place of worship or faith community
- your local community center, YMCA, or YWCA

If the first person you reach out to isn't as helpful as you'd like, don't give up. Keep looking until you find an adult who listens.

Dealing with change

Do you live in a "typical" family? With people constantly on the move from one place to another and with one out of every two marriages ending in divorce, you live in a time when practically any family configuration could be considered typical. Step-families, single-parent homes, adoptive families, shared custody situations, blended families, extended families, families separated by geography—all of these arrangements are typical for many teens at one time or another. In a word, what's typical when it comes to family life is *change.* This doesn't mean that adjusting from one to another of these situations is simple. In most cases, families dealing with big life changes are families dealing with stress.

SAM was 14 and going into ninth grade, another big change. After his parents got divorced last year, his dad moved about an hour away and Sam could only see him every other weekend. That was bad enough, but his mom married Jeff a couple of months ago, and now Jeff's younger sons, Jon and Eric, were "family."

Sam thought Eric and Jon were okay, but they were really different from him and he didn't feel comfortable hanging around them at home. Both Eric and Jon were science heads, while Sam liked art and cartooning, and spending time outdoors with his dog, Clancy. Science stuff was scattered everywhere he looked: microscopes, magnifiers, rocks, dead bugs. "This is so unfair!" thought Sam. "It's like an invasion."

But Sam wasn't the type of person who could easily express his feelings, even the positive ones. He knew he was stressed, but he hadn't talked with his mother because she seemed so happy. He didn't want to bring her down or make her feel like he was being a pain. And he definitely didn't want her to start loving him less, which he worried might happen now that she had two other kids in her life.

On Saturday morning, Sam woke early and had the whole day planned out. He would take Clancy down to the beach so they could run around. But at breakfast, Mom said, "The science museum opens in an hour. What do you say—are you guys interested?"

Jon and Eric jumped up and yelled, "Yeah!"

Sam looked at his mom in disbelief. "I thought you said it was okay to go to the beach."

"I know," she admitted, "but Jon and Eric love the science museum. And I thought it would be nice for all of us to do something together with the boys, as a family."

Whenever his mom used the phrase "the boys," Sam cringed.

"I'm one of the boys too!" he shouted. "And I hate science." Then leaping to his feet he added hotly, "We never did that kind of stuff before!" He ran outside, and Clancy followed.

Sam knew he was stressed and that he shouldn't have run off, but he couldn't help it. He turned around and saw his mom in the doorway, looking upset. "Good," he thought. "Serves her right."

Then he remembered some things he'd learned about handling stress. He took a couple of deep breaths and started to pull himself together. When Clancy pressed against Sam's legs, Sam felt himself starting to relax.

Tool #1:
breathing,
see page
54.

He noticed his mom walking toward him. "What should I say?" he wondered. He began to think about what was really bothering him, and he realized it wasn't just the science museum. It was everything else too. He could only see Dad a couple times a month, and Mom wasn't just his mom anymore. He realized he didn't like sharing. Now that he was a little calmer, he saw that he had never talked to his mom about all these feelings.

Tool #2:
thinking,
see page
57.

His mom reached him and asked, "Will you sit with me a minute?" They both sat down on the curb.

"What's up?" she asked.

He considered what to say. "Them or me, Mom. You choose," was one thought. But that sounded too dramatic. He thought about saying, "Nothing's wrong, I guess we'll do what you want today." Then he thought about not saying a word—just giving Mom the old silent treatment—which felt like the easiest thing to do. But Sam realized that it wouldn't actually fix anything.

Finally, he decided to just be honest. "I don't feel good saying this, but the whole 'new happy family thing' is really hard for me."

Tool #4:
choosing,
see page
61.

"I've noticed, Sam, and that makes it hard for me too. Maybe you never knew this, but I've always kind of wanted a big family—you know, brothers and sisters for you—but it didn't quite work out that way, until now."

"But Mom, when you call Jon and Eric 'the boys,' I feel like I don't mean as much to you anymore."

"You mean everything to me, and I'll try to show that more. And I'm sorry if I hurt you."

"Thanks," said Sam. "So, what about the museum?"

"We don't have to go," said his mom. "Maybe Eric and Jon would like the beach too. They already look up to you as a big brother. What do you think about asking them to join you?"

"I'll think about it," said Sam.

"That's all I'm asking," said his mom. "Just think about it and continue talking to me about what you're feeling. I love you, Sam, and I don't ever want to lose this."

"Me either," Sam replied with a smile.

Facing change isn't easy, even when the changes are *good* ones. Change is a stressor for most people. When your life goes in a different direction, you may have to adjust to new people, places, and expectations. Some transitions take an emotional toll, especially in the case of a death, divorce, or separation. You may feel like you're losing your family, your home, and your sense of security. It may seem as if your whole world has turned upside down and that you can't get back on your feet again.

Find someone—your dad, mom, or another adult—who will listen and help you through this transition. Talk to your friends too. Many of them have probably been through tough family situations, and they'll relate to how you feel. Seek out other sources of support, if needed. Chapter 10 includes information on seeing a counselor or joining a support group.

 THINK ABOUT IT: In Sam's story, he uses some of the tools from the get-back-in-balance tool kit (see Chapter 4). How might he begin to use tool #3, *flexing?* What character traits or behaviors might Sam work on to improve his relationship with his mom?

 WRITE ABOUT IT: What is the biggest change you've faced in your life? How did you feel when it took place? How have you dealt with it? What did you learn about yourself?

Family meetings (a stress buster at home)

When problems don't get resolved, they can turn into boomerang issues that just keep coming back around again. Talking is a great way to start resolving problems at home, but it helps to have a plan for *how* to talk. That's where family meetings come in handy. They can help your family practice good communication skills and get back on track.

Start by telling the adults in your family that you think having regular meetings will help everyone talk through issues together. This will show that you're serious about talking and willing to take the lead. To schedule the first meeting, pick a time when everyone is likely to be in a relatively good mood, and then put the date on the family calendar. Decide ahead of time what the topic of the meeting will be. For example, you may want to talk about one particular hot-button issue that affects everyone in  the family. Or, you may decide to have a general meeting in which each person can bring up something that's stressing him or her out. Everyone should have a chance to talk and be heard. Your family may even choose to pass an object of some sort to the speaker so there's no confusion about who "has the floor."

When it's your turn to talk, follow these guidelines:

Know your goal. What do you want? Knowing this ahead of time is crucial, so define your goal and make sure it's realistic. It never helps to compare your family to other families or talk about what your friends' parents let them do. Instead, state your goal positively: "I've been thinking about how I could use some extra money to buy some of the things I need, like clothes. I'm really lucky that you give me an allowance, but I'm wondering if you might think about raising it. I'm willing to do more chores. I've even thought about getting a part-time job, but with all the homework I have to do, I'm not sure I have time. Would you consider giving me a higher allowance?"

Measure your words. If you're bringing up a tough issue and you know there's a chance that a family member will feel accused or attacked, think carefully about what to say. If you use words like "You always" or "You never," you're going to push that person's buttons and trigger a stress response. Try "I messages" instead by sharing your own feelings without blame. You might say, "I feel like you don't trust me as much as I need you to, and I'm wondering what's going on."

Stay calm. Remember your tools from Chapter 4? Use them in a family meeting to keep a cool head. If the meeting gets too stressful and you need a break, just say, "I could use a break. Can I have a few minutes?" Come back when you're calmer and ready to talk.

When it's somebody else's turn to talk:

Listen. It takes 100 percent of your attention to really listen when someone else is talking. Maintaining eye contact as much as possible shows the speaker that you're hearing what's being said. That's what you want when it's your turn, right? So hang in there and make sure you're willing to give what everyone deserves—being listened to with an open heart and an open mind.

Watch your body language. Even when you aren't speaking, you still communicate through body language. If your arms and legs are crossed and you're frowning or rolling your eyes, you're silently communicating that you're not really open to what the other person is saying. When people feel judged, their stress levels go up and communication breaks down.

Reflect back what you've heard. Try to understand the feelings behind the words, and then use your own words to "play back" what's been said. For example, "What I hear you saying is that you worry about me when I'm out past my curfew." This shows you've really made an effort to hear the other person's point of view. When the speaker is assured that the listener "got it," then everyone's stress level goes down and you start making real progress in resolving conflicts.

Compromise and make a plan. If the issue is that you don't like it when your parents constantly ask, "Have you finished your homework yet?" then talk about what you want and what you're willing to give in order to get it. For example, "I want to be trusted to take care of my homework on my own. I want to show you I can do it. If I set up a homework schedule, can you trust me to follow it and assume I've done what I need to do without asking me?"

How often do you need a family meeting? Some families only call meetings when there's a major issue to discuss. Others hold them on a regular basis to clear the air. Still others make a routine of talking over dinner, instead of during scheduled meetings. Do whatever works for you. The important thing is to communicate openly and share your feelings, listen to what others have to say, and work together to solve problems successfully. That's going to go a long way toward helping your family become less stressed.

6

Friends and Supporters

Friends are as important as air, water, and food. Now that you're a teen, the role your friends play takes on a deeper meaning. Although your family may still be your main source of love and support, your friends are probably the people you spend the most time with. Even outside of school, you probably want to hang with them more than with your mom or dad. That's natural. Who else but your friends understand how awesome your crush is, how aggravating the new basketball coach is, or how scared you are about your history final? Plus, your friends know how to make you laugh and probably share many of your interests. They're your greatest source of fun and, well, *friendship.*

If you took a close look at your friendships, what would you discover? Do you have a best friend? One or two close friends you spend most of your time with? A whole group of buddies you hang out with nearly every day? When it comes to how many friends you've got, there's no magic number. More important, how do you *feel* when you're with them? Relaxed? Safe? Free to be who you are? Real friends accept you for *you.* You don't have to worry about fitting in with them, hiding your true self, or saying the "right" thing. With a real friend, you can take your shoes off, and even if your sock has a hole in it or you've got a zit on your chin, your friend doesn't care.

Good Friends...

☐ respect you

☐ let you talk, and listen to what you have to say

☐ can be trusted

☐ tell you the truth

☐ help you de-stress

☐ stand by you and stick up for you

☐ don't blow you off

☐ let you vent when needed

☐ give you an honest opinion when asked

☐ respect your privacy and keep things confidential

☐ don't pressure you to do things you don't want to do

☐ are good for your mind and your spirit

Look at the list above and ask yourself if your closest friends fit that profile. You should be able to count on them when you need something, whether it's a good laugh, a small favor, or a shoulder to cry on. Are they really there for you? Are *you* there for *them?* It goes without saying that part of having a good friend is *being* one. The healthiest and most balanced friendships are the ones in which trust, respect, and understanding go both ways.

Your support network

Throughout this book, you've learned ways to handle stress and get back in balance. Many of the techniques, such as taking better care of your body and using your stress-busting tools, can mostly be done on your own. But not everything you do to get back in balance is a solo act—you still need your friends. Building a support network is essential to a less stressful lifestyle and to your growth as a person. Here's an activity to help you see how *your* network looks:

Your Social Circle

1. Get some unlined paper and a pen or pencil.

2. Draw a small circle in the center of the paper and label the circle, "Me."

3. Around the "Me" circle, write the name of your best friend, if you have one, and your other closest friends. Put a circle around each name.

4. Around those, write the names of other people you're friendly with but not as close to. (For example, teammates, friends of friends, people you talk to in class but don't spend a lot of time with.) Circle each of these names.

5. Before continuing, take a look at your circles. Does it feel good to know that you've got these people in your life? Do you wish you had more names to add?

6. Next, think about the level of support you get from each person whose name is circled. For anyone who is "very helpful," draw double lines from your circle to his or hers. People who are "somewhat helpful" get a single line connecting their circle to yours. If you've got people in your network who are "sometimes helpful but often not," draw a wavy line between you. For people who are "not at all helpful" or "cause more problems," draw a connecting line with an "X" through it.

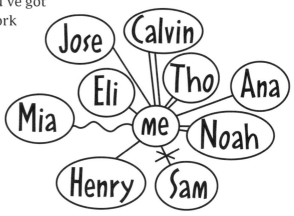

When you're done, ask yourself:

- Who truly supports me? How do I know?
- Who doesn't support me? Why not?
- If my biggest supporters were to draw their own social circle, would *I* be listed as one of *their* supporters?
- Are some of the people I hang out with making my life more difficult?
- Do I need to work on building a network of true supporters who really help me?
- If I'd drawn this map six months ago, would it look the same? How about a year ago? What has changed?

Some of your relationships are more important than others. You spend more time with certain friends, and they have more of an emotional impact on your life. The question is, are those relationships balanced, or do they add to your stress?

Maybe after doing the above exercise, you realized that you don't have many friends or that the friends you *do* have aren't very supportive. Either way, it's stressful. But there are definitely steps you can take to improve your situation. Think about ways to meet more people. Could you:

- join a team or club at school or in your community?
- join the YMCA or YWCA?
- get involved in a youth program at a place of worship?
- check out teen programming through your public library?
- get a part-time after-school job?
- explore what your local community center has to offer?
- volunteer with other teens at an animal shelter or for a political campaign?

Most likely, new friends aren't just going to show up on your doorstep. You have to put yourself out there and talk to people, even if you're nervous at first. Enjoy the process of getting to know people—the rewards are huge. Friendships can boost your confidence, lower your stress levels, and help you get more out of life.

 THINK ABOUT IT: If you want to get closer to the friends you already have, start by making yourself more available to them. Do a better job of listening to your friends' stories, problems, and jokes. Sometimes, *you* have take the lead in strengthening your friendships. You'll be glad you did.

TALK ABOUT IT: Do you feel like you can talk to your friends about almost anything? If your friends don't usually share their problems with you and you want them to open up more, what might you do to get the ball rolling? (Tip: You could say, "I want you to know that you can trust me. If you ever want to talk about stuff, just let me know.") If you feel like opening up first, you could start a conversation this way, "Something's been bothering me lately, and I really need someone to talk to. Do you have time to listen?"

TAKE IT INTO THE REAL WORLD: Each day for the next week at school, say hi to at least three people you've never spoken to before. Smile, make eye contact, and be friendly. At the end of the week, reflect on what happened. What kinds of responses did you get? How did you feel inside? Did anything change for you?

The ups and downs of friendship

Even when you know who your most trusted friends are and you can turn to each other for support, problems may still come up. Best buddies can have different temperaments and are bound to have conflicting opinions once in a while. At times, you may push each other's buttons without even realizing it.

Because your friends are so important day to day, it's especially difficult when one of them happens to be a stressor for you. You may feel angry or disappointed if someone you're supposed to be able to count on isn't there for you. Or, you might feel hurt if a friend has betrayed you. In the midst of it all, you may think, "No one else knows and understands everything about me. Who will I hang out with now?"

What are some conflicts you've had with a friend?

"I asked my friend for a sheet of paper, and he said, 'No! What, are you too poor to buy one?' I argued, but finally I just said, 'Whatever,' and asked someone else. The next day, he apologized and said he was just in a bad mood because his uncle died. So I forgave him."
—Tim, 12

"My best guy friend is really sweet when we're alone, but when his friends are around he acts like a jerk."
—Lara, 14

"My best friend used to be confident and outgoing. Now he seems bored and quiet. I want to stay friends, but he's acting like he doesn't. I'm also worried about why he's like this."
—Isaac, 16

"I feel like my three close friends are smothering me and not letting me become friends with other people."
—Imogine, 15

"I'm not sure how long my best friend and I can stay friends. We're both so argumentative. When I brought this up to him, he got mad. Hence, another debate."
—Douglas, 18

"One of my friends noticed that I put myself down a lot, and she told a few other friends. Now they all try to help me, but it's just worse. I feel like I'm being watched or babysat all the time."
—Brenda, 14

"I was in a fight with my old best friend, and I told her I didn't want to be her friend anymore. I was jealous of her new friend. I'm sad because I miss her, and we burned a bridge. We haven't really talked since."
—Kikki, 12

Even the closest friendships aren't perfect. You might have mis-understandings, disagreements, or even big fights. These are often fueled by competition or jealousy, which can put distance between friends. As soon as you recognize that something's not right between you and a friend, don't ignore it. Take some time to calm down, think about what's going on, and make good choices about what to do. What's best for you? What's best for the friendship?

You might also need your "get-back-in-balance tool kit" (see page 53). Real friendships are worth holding on to, even though you may feel like screaming at your friend or never talking to him or her again. Instead, talk calmly about whatever is stressing you out. Many teens (and adults, for that matter) find it difficult to start these conversations. Sometimes, it seems easier to avoid the issue, ignore a friend, or talk behind his or her back. These actions won't get your friendship back on track—in most cases, they'll only lead to hard feelings. You and your friend may actually grow closer if you work through conflicts, instead of pretending they don't exist or letting them sabotage the relationship.

TAKE IT INTO THE REAL WORLD: Check out the tips on pages 84–86 in the section on family meetings—they work for friends too! You'll find ideas for bringing up difficult subjects and communicating respectfully. If you're not having any conflicts with a friend, that's great—but you can still do something to make your friendship stronger. You might write your friend a note or open up about something that's on your mind. You have to nurture a friendship to help it grow.

One thing that's always important to remember is the power of forgiveness. If you've done something that hurt a friend and you haven't apologized yet, why not do it today? You'll feel better when you say you're sorry and make amends. If you're holding a grudge against a friend who has hurt you, you're only increasing your own stress. Do yourself a favor by consciously choosing to forgive that person. It doesn't mean you have to *forget* about what happened, but you can put the hurt behind you and move on. By choosing not to devote any more time to hurt and resentment, you'll have energy to focus on the positives in your life.

When a friendship ends

KALLI had been away at camp for most of the summer, and Roxanne, her best friend, really missed her. One day, Roxanne was at the mall and ran into Kalli's mom, who greeted her warmly.

"Roxanne," she said, "When are you coming over? We've missed you this summer."

"I'll be there the minute Kalli gets back," Roxanne answered.

"But—" Kalli's mom said, looking confused. "Kalli's been home for two weeks. Didn't she call you?"

Now it was Roxanne's turn to be confused. How could Kalli be home for two whole weeks without calling? Roxanne had thought it was a little strange that Kalli hadn't sent her any postcards from camp or replied to any letters she'd written. Roxanne had told herself that Kalli didn't have time to write. But now she wasn't so sure.

"Um, I have to go," she mumbled to Kalli's mom, feeling the sting of tears in her eyes.

Has anything like this happened to you? Did a friend do something you thought was out of line? Has a friendship of yours ever faded away or ended abruptly? When friendships fall apart, it helps to get some perspective. Don't assume that a friend has created distance because he or she:

- hates you now
- never really liked you
- was a jerk to begin with
- doesn't care about the friendship and the good times you've had

The change in a friendship may not be about *you* at all, and the situation will only stress you out more if you assume everything is your fault. Maybe your friend has developed some new interests, like sports or a club, or is spending more time with a different group. People sometimes grow into new relationships as they outgrow old ones. It might be natural for this to happen, but it can still be difficult if you're the friend who's been left behind. This is doubly hard if you've been dumped or treated poorly by someone who you thought cared about you.

When **ROXANNE** got home from the mall, the first thing she did was to try to breathe and calm down. She was stressed out and, she admitted to herself, really mad at Kalli. "How can she treat me this way?" she wondered.

Tool #1: breathing, see page 54.

She went to her room and thought about the situation. She realized she wanted to talk to someone and get some advice. "Well, obviously I can't talk to Kalli . . . yet anyway." So, she went to find her dad. "I need to talk to you, Dad," she said. "Something's going on, and I don't know what to do."

Tool #2: thinking, see page 57.

Her dad sat beside her on the couch and listened as Roxanne told him the whole story of how Kalli hadn't written to her from camp. Roxanne also told him how she'd just found out that Kalli had already been home for a couple of weeks. "She hasn't called, Dad. I don't think she wants to be friends any more."

"What do you want to do about it?" her dad asked.

Roxanne sighed. "I guess I'll call her. I think she owes me an explanation."

Tool #4: choosing, see page 61.

As she picked up the phone, Roxanne felt shaky, and her palms were sweaty. When Kalli answered, Roxanne got right to the point.

"Kalli," she said, "I know you've been home for a while, and you haven't called. I want to know what's up."

There was a long silence on the other end. Then Kalli finally said, "I'm sorry. I should have written to you. When I got home, I didn't know what to say. A lot has changed for me. I have new friends now. I guess . . . what I'm saying is that I don't feel as close to you anymore. I don't want to spend as much time together."

Roxanne took a deep breath and tried to stay calm. "This is pretty much what I was expecting to hear," she thought. Part of her wanted to yell or slam down the phone in Kalli's ear, but she reminded herself to stay calm.

"What do you mean a lot has changed for you?" Roxanne asked.

Kalli sighed. "Well, you know, there's soccer. You're not on the team, and my teammates and I spend a lot of time together after school and at tournaments and stuff. Some of us went to summer soccer camp together. It's hard for me to make time for everything and everyone. I'm sorry."

"Okay, Kalli," Roxanne said. "I understand what you're saying. I just wish you had told me earlier. Our friendship was important to me, and I'm sorry you don't feel the same way about it anymore."

As they said good-bye, Roxanne felt sad and disappointed. But she was also proud of the way she'd handled the situation. She went to tell her dad about the conversation. She knew he'd understand.

The end of a friendship can be painful and stressful. It's a good idea to talk to someone about what you're going through, even if you feel like no one would understand. Reach out to your other friends, a sibling, a parent, or somebody you trust so that you won't have to be alone as you go through this experience. Take good care of yourself by continuing to exercise, eat right, rest, and stay involved in activities you enjoy. And, though you may feel sad at times, keep your heart and mind open to new friendships.

 WRITE ABOUT IT: Use your journal to express your feelings, to vent, or even to write your friend a letter about how you feel (don't send the letter, though). Afterward, do something to lift your mood, like spending time with people who care about you.

TALK ABOUT IT: Interview a parent or another trusted adult about the friends they had when they were your age. Some questions to ask might include: How did those friendships turn out? How would you feel if you saw your old friends again? What advice do you have about being a good friend?

How a mentor can help

When you hear the word *mentor,* what comes to mind? Maybe a role model who inspires others to go after their dreams, or a trusted adult who offers wisdom and guidance to a young person in need? A mentor can be all these things and more.

A mentor is basically a caring adult or an older teen who's willing to spend one-on-one time with you and guide you in reaching your fullest potential. If you don't already have a mentor, consider finding one. He or she can become an essential part of your growing network of support.

Who might be a mentor for you? How about a parent, relative, teacher, coach, neighbor, or community member? Other options include older cousins or peers. Start by asking adults you already know and trust for help in learning more about mentors. Talk to people at your school, community center, or place of worship. You might also try a national organization that screens and trains mentors, including the YMCA, YWCA, or Big Brothers Big Sisters (you'll find their contact info on pages 151–153).

The key is to find someone who believes in you and wants to see you succeed. Maybe you already have someone in mind, but if not, make a list of potential mentors. By the way, you don't have to look for just *one* mentor—you could have several, if you'd like. The more caring people you've got in your corner the better.

Research shows that teens need supportive people in their lives to turn to for advice. It's helpful to get an older person's perspective on issues you face every day. This can make the process of growing up a little smoother. But how can your mentor help you manage stress? He or she might:

- talk to you about your personal stressors
- listen to your feelings or problems
- offer emotional support
- share life experiences
- help you better understand your own temperament or the behaviors/attitudes you might work on
- support you as you learn to exercise and eat right for better health
- help you face and break free from your stress traps
- guide you in making positive choices
- spend time doing your favorite stress-relieving activities with you
- cheer you on as you go for your goals
- point to further resources if you're dealing with more stress than you can handle

 TALK ABOUT IT: Ask a parent or grandparent if he or she ever had a mentor. How was that person helpful and supportive?

It may feel a little scary to seek out a mentor and then ask that person to take on a bigger role in your life. Know that many adults feel *honored* to be mentors, if given the chance. Lots of people care about you, value you for who you are, and want to help you succeed—but you might have to make the first move. So, what are you waiting for?

dating jobs family pressure

cliques homework identity tests

bullying friends

The Boyfriend/ Girlfriend Zone

There's an old song about how love "makes the world go 'round." You don't have to be Einstein to know that love has nothing to do with the Earth's rotation, but it's true that falling in love has inspired people all over the world throughout history. One of the more exciting parts of being a teen is discovering love and waking up to the fact that you've got sexual feelings. In addition to the physical thrill of being kissed, held, or wanted by someone special, there are the emotional highs of being together, expressing feelings, sharing laughter, and just having fun.

Q & A

What kind of support do you get (or want) from a boyfriend or girlfriend?

"My girlfriend was the only one I could talk to about stuff when my granddad died."
—Mitchell, 16

"When my boyfriend is going through a lot at home, I always try to be there for him like he has for me."
—Emily, 16

"I really want a boyfriend who will be there for me every day of my life, encourage me to become a better person, and help me find out who I am."
—Maeve, 14

"I really want to be with someone and share feelings and secrets."
—Roberto, 14

"My boyfriend cheers me up when I'm down."
—Carina, 16

"My boyfriend is so sweet, and he sticks up for me, and he is always there for me, making sure I'm okay and stuff."
—Krista, 13

"The perfect girlfriend is one who is always proud of me, and she isn't afraid to say 'I love you.'"
—Lee, 15

"I wish I had a girlfriend who knows what I'm going through, so I could talk to her about all my problems."
—Tony, 13

"Whenever I was crying, my boyfriend would stay on the phone and listen to me."
—Brianna, 14

"I want a girlfriend who says, 'I respect that you have your own ideas and beliefs,' even if they are different from hers."
—Gerald, 17

There's no question about it, boyfriend/girlfriend (bf/gf)* relationships can be absolutely great but, not surprisingly, they can also be a source of stress. For example, maybe:

- you're attracted to someone but you're not sure how to make your feelings known
- you can barely think straight when you're around your crush and always seem to say the wrong thing
- you've never had a crush on anyone and you're wondering if that's normal (it is)

---

*To keep it simple, we use the abbreviation bf/gf to mean boyfriend or girlfriend.

- you're unsure of your sexual identity
- you're in a relationship but you're not sure it feels right for you
- you were in a relationship but you broke up, and now you're still trying to get over it

You may not have experienced any of these emotional ups and downs yet, but chances are good that before you leave high school, you *will* have. Many teens spend a lot of time stressing and obsessing about falling in love. That's natural. But it's a tough balancing act when you're trying to stay on top of your work at school, stay connected to your family and friends, *and* find or keep a bf/gf too.

When it comes to the bf/gf zone, you can choose not to put so much pressure on yourself. In fact, what you may need even more than a bf/gf is the chance to build healthy *friend*ships with girls and guys. At this point in your life, friendships are often more meaningful than romantic relationships, and they usually last longer too (read more about friendships in Chapter 6). Friendships can also help you learn important things about yourself and your values. If you focus on widening your circle of friends and being a good friend to the ones you've already got, you may feel less pressure to find a bf/gf. Then later, when the time is right for you and you meet someone special, you may discover that you're more self-assured and relationship ready.

The Brain/Love Connection

According to a 2005 study, love and attraction can do a number on the brain. Scientists studied people in the early stages of love and learned that the majority of these Romeos and Juliets experienced increased energy, euphoria (extreme happiness), a loss of appetite, sleeplessness, and constant thoughts about their love interest. Looking at brain scans, the scientists noticed that the part of the brain that focuses on rewards and motivation had gone into high gear.

In fact, this area of the brain and the chemicals it produces are the same ones that get activated for people who are addicted to gambling or drugs. This new research suggests that romantic love sparks an intense need for reward—in this case, the human drive to win the affection of a potential mate. The drive is so strong that it knocks you completely off-balance. (No wonder it's so hard to think about anything but your crush and how you might impress him or her!) When those passionate feelings are ignited, fasten your seatbelt. The ride may be wild, so take it slow and don't forget to take care of yourself.

Maybe you're already in a bf/gf relationship and learning firsthand about the highs and lows of being in love. What's at the core of your relationship, besides physical attraction? How about friendship? (That's why the word *friend* is half of "boyfriend" and "girlfriend.") It doesn't mean you had to be friends first—just that you accept each other's unique qualities and treat each other as well as you'd treat your best friends. If your bf/gf isn't someone you'd want as a friend, that could be a warning sign of an unhealthy relationship.

THINK ABOUT IT: Do you and your bf/gf respect and trust each other? Can you really talk about stuff that matters? What stresses you out most about your bf/gf? What do you usually do about that? (Check out the stress-busting tools in Chapter 4 if you need help.)

Relationship red flags (and what to do)

Every healthy relationship is based on two-way trust and respect. If you truly understand this is what you deserve and you're willing to speak up when you're not getting it, you'll be in a better position to evaluate how healthy your relationship is.

In this book, we've talked a lot about *balance.* A balanced relationship is one in which both people think of each other as equals and act accordingly. If one person feels more important, loved, or in charge, then the relationship is unequal, unbalanced, and unhealthy—and that means trouble.

But many people don't recognize problems in their own relationships. Maybe they're so in love or infatuated that they miss the warning signs. Maybe they think that what they have is as good as it gets because they haven't dated much and have no basis for comparison. Or, perhaps they believe that even an unbalanced relationship is better than no relationship at all. (It isn't!) Feeling like this may make it hard to see that the relationship has become a major stressor in their lives.

TALK ABOUT IT: Are you and your bf/gf part of each other's support network? (See page 88.) How have you shown your support? What opportunities have you missed to give each other support? Talk this over.

Red flags are warnings that your relationship isn't everything it could be. In some cases, those uncomfortable moments, feelings, or events are little signs that you may need to stand up for yourself more often, communicate better, or set some new ground rules for the relationship. In other cases, certain red flags are much more serious, especially ones that point to abuse (see pages 107–109 for more information).

Pressure

Romantic relationships come with their own set of pressures, mostly involving any form of intimacy, including sex. You probably know from a parent or a school health course that sex includes physical risks like unwanted pregnancy or sexually transmitted diseases (STDs). But there are potential emotional risks too, such as feeling disappointed in yourself, feeling distant from your partner, and/or regretting what happened. Because the physical and emotional consequences of sex can be stressful, especially if you're a teen, you want to be sure you're making good decisions.

If you're not ready to have sex, that's your choice and no one else's. You don't have to do anything that you're not ready for. But what if your bf/gf is putting on the pressure? You might hear stuff like, "Everybody else is doing it, why not us?" or "But I thought you loved me!" When someone pressures you, especially someone you care about, it's a lot harder to think clearly—but not impossible. You still have *choices.* Ultimately, you have to do what's right for you, even if it's not what your partner wants or expects. In healthy relationships, both partners are equals. That means you have a right to stand up for what you want and need—and be heard.

The choice to have sex is a very personal and private one. It can be a life-altering decision. Don't wait to make this choice until you're in the heat of the moment; otherwise, you may end up regretting your decision and asking yourself, "What was I *thinking?*" Instead, talk to an adult you trust about your values and what's important to you. Also, get accurate information about sex and the consequences of physical intimacy. You can go to a parent or guardian, a teacher, a doctor, or the school counselor. Although it may stress you out to ask questions about sex, it's even *more* stressful when you just don't have the answers you need and deserve.

 TAKE IT INTO THE REAL WORLD: Talking about how you feel is a mature way for you and your bf/gf to understand each other better. Have a calm, respectful conversation about sex without any pressure to *do* anything. Share your point of view and listen to what your bf/gf has to say.

If your bf/gf pressures you to go further than you're ready to and won't back off, that's not a good sign. Even if you've already been sexually active before, you always have the choice to say no. Tell your bf/gf that you want to take it slow and that he or she has to respect your decision. If that doesn't work, it's time to break up and move on.

Conflict

You already know how challenging it can be to keep your own balance day to day. When your bf/gf is involved, situations become more complex. You have someone else's feelings and needs to consider. It can be especially frustrating if your bf/gf disagrees with you or doesn't want the same things you want.

When conflicts heat up, one or both of you might lash out, shut down, or take off. A lot depends on your individual temperaments and your personal reactions to stress. You may already know that yelling or refusing to talk doesn't get you far. Resolving a conflict means getting to the bottom of it once and for all, but for a lot of people, that's easier said than done. Some couples break up because they don't know how to talk things out. Others get so caught up in the drama of fighting that they forget that the relationship is supposed to be about growing closer. Still others swallow their anger and pretend nothing's wrong—and nothing gets resolved.

When you have a disagreement with your bf/gf, how do you handle it? Yelling? Blaming? The silent treatment? Talking? Listening? Compromising? It takes two people to fight and two to make the peace. Each person involved has to be part of the process. If you're both willing to try, then here are some tips for problem solving.

Problem: You're too upset to talk without screaming, crying, or threatening to break up.

How to handle it: Don't talk about it yet. Cool off first.

Stay calm: It's impossible to work out a conflict when you're really upset. If you can't control your emotions, spend some time by yourself. It may help to take some re-centering breaths (that's get-back-in-balance tool #1; see page 53). Another option is to do something physical. Go for a walk or run, bike, do sit-ups or push-ups—anything to get your body in motion. For some people, listening to music or taking a long shower is a de-stressor. Write in your journal, if you'd like—whatever helps you calm down.

* * *

Problem: Everyone else is talking about the fight between you and your bf/gf.

How to handle it: It's one thing if your friends are trying to be supportive—it's another thing if people are choosing sides and making your fight worse. Don't worry about what other people think or let them interfere. Focus instead on what you and your bf/gf can do to work it out.

Talk one on one: Pick a place that's private and quiet. Talking face to face is best, but if that's not possible, do it over the phone. Before the conversation, take a look at the guidelines for better communication in Chapter 5 (see pages 84–86).

* * *

Problem: You and your bf/gf keep blaming each other for whatever happened.

How to handle it: You can consciously choose to take a different approach. Instead of blaming, try to look at the conflict from your bf/gf's point of view and ask yourself what role you played.

See each other's side: It's always easier to point a finger than to actually try to work problems out. But when you're resolving a conflict, there's no room for blame. Work together to figure out how each person contributed to the conflict (because *both* of you probably did). Each of you should answer these questions out loud: *What did I say or do that made you angry/stressed? What could I have done differently?* Next, consider an apology, a compromise, or both.

* * *

Problem: You get in the same old arguments again and again.

How to handle it: Ask yourself what's really going on. Are you and your bf/gf really ready for this relationship? Is one of you more mature than the other one? Or, is it more about a clash of temperament?

Try to flex: You can't control your bf/gf's behavior, but you can definitely change your own. And that, in turn, might encourage your bf/gf to behave differently toward you. Look at your temperament and see if any aspect of it might be getting in your way (see pages 25–29 for more on temperament). For example, maybe you're a bit stubborn or you like to be right, in which case it may be difficult for you to see the other person's point of view or admit to a mistake. What if you were to flex this trait a little bit each day? Or, what if you were to consciously flex during your next disagreement with your bf/gf? You might be amazed at how well this works. For more on flexing, see pages 59–61.

* * *

If you try all of these ideas and the conflicts continue, it's time to ask yourself if the relationship is worth all the stress it's causing you. Talk to family and friends to get their perspectives and support.

Control

At 16, **JANELLE** was on the shy side and lacked self-confidence. She'd had crushes on guys before, but she hadn't ever let them know how she felt. None of them ever seemed to notice anyway. Then, four months ago, she met Nick. He was really sweet in the beginning, calling her all the time, buying her gifts, and taking her out. She was convinced she had found her true love.

But lately, Nick was spending most of his time with a new group of friends and Janelle sat at home a lot, waiting by the phone. Nick had told her that he wanted her to be there whenever he called—not out somewhere so he couldn't meet up with her easily when he wanted to. Even though her friends kept asking her to spend time with them, Janelle stayed home thinking Nick might call.

Then, Nick started to get even more "protective." He told Janelle he didn't like it that she was friends with other guys. "You're mine," he said.

"I don't want other guys looking at you." At first, Janelle was flattered, and she even thought it was kind of cool that Nick was the jealous type.

Some of Janelle's friends tried to talk to her about what was going on. "Why do you stay with him?" they asked.

Janelle tried to explain. "You don't understand. He's actually really sweet, and he cares about me. And I love him."

But one day, she was outside of school waiting for Nick to walk home with her. She was talking to Rafael, a boy she'd known for years who already had a girlfriend. They were just talking about algebra, but Nick got really mad. He came up behind Janelle and pushed her. She bumped right into Rafael, and that hurt.

"Whoa," Rafael said to Nick. "Relax, man."

Nick got in his face and told him to keep away from Janelle. Then he grabbed her by the hand and pulled her away. She followed, trying to hold back tears. When Nick saw that she was about to cry, he just laughed. That hurt Janelle even more.

Nick is not only controlling but violent. Many of his actions are red flags: extreme jealousy, not letting Janelle talk to other guys, making her wait by the phone, lashing out at people who talk to her, hurting her physically, and laughing at her when she cries. His relationship with Janelle is abusive and becoming more dangerous for her every day. Janelle feels unsure about how to change the situation, but the longer she stays in the relationship, the more control Nick gets.

An abusive relationship is incredibly confusing and stressful. The mistreatment may occur infrequently or at random. One minute the abuser may be sweet, and the very next he or she may lash out with angry words or physical violence. Once someone is caught in an abusive relationship, it can be very hard to break free.

If you're in a situation like this, know that you *can* get out. To take care of yourself right now, go to an adult. Don't try to talk to your bf/gf, because he or she could get violent. Right now, your safety is more important. There are hotlines you can call if you can't go to a trusted adult at this time. Contact the National Center for Victims of Crime (NCVC) at 1-800-FYI-CALL (1-800-394-2255) for support. The National Domestic Violence Hotline also offers crisis intervention for abuse victims; call 1-800-799-SAFE (1-800-799-7233). For information on seeking adult help, see Chapter 10.

When Janelle got home, **NICK** said, "I'll call you later." He acted like nothing had happened. When he kissed her good-bye, Janelle felt sick to her stomach. She decided enough was enough.

She locked the apartment door behind her and went to find her mom. Janelle decided to tell her everything about Nick, even though she knew her mom would be upset. Making that decision felt like a huge weight off her shoulders. She took a few deep breaths and said, "Mom, I need help. Nick pushed me, and he acts like he owns me or something. I want to break up with him, but I'm afraid of what he might do."

Her mom reached out and hugged her. "I'm so glad you told me," she said. "I want you to be safe, and I'll do whatever I can to help."

* * *

Of course, not all bf/gf relationships are stressful and unhealthy. In many ways, the bf/gf zone is a world of wonderful new possibilities. You can learn so much about your emotions, girls/guys, your views on sexuality, and how to care for someone more deeply than you ever have before. Having a bf/gf also provides great opportunities to give and get support.

But healthy, balanced relationships don't happen by accident or by luck. They develop from the choices you make. You can always choose to talk from your heart and to listen with an open mind. You can also share what you've learned in this book about staying in balance. Then, the next time you or your bf/gf feels stressed, you can help each other out. It takes two people to make a relationship, and the same two to make it *great.*

8

Stress Less at School

Tough classes, high expectations from parents, a homework load, a schedule that leaves you no time for yourself—you don't need us to tell you that school can be really stressful. In fact, it's the #1 stressor for most teens. And because it might be the center of your social life too, you may have some other school-related issues to deal with, including cliques, peer pressure, popularity, and how you fit into the mix.

The first step to feeling better about school may be to flex your point of view. Maybe you experience school as an endless chore, a pressure cooker, or a scene of repeated failures and humiliations. What if, on the other hand, you tried viewing going to school as a kind of role-playing game? (Why not?) Like a game, school provides all sorts of challenges to be met. You learn to overcome obstacles and frequently have to prove yourself through tests of knowledge and skill. For each level of success you achieve, you're awarded points and grades. Then, after years of jumping through the rings of fire, you get a prize—a diploma, your ticket to the future. With that ticket in hand, you've got more power to create the kind of life you want.

Think of school as a game if it helps you, and then look at some ways you can play that game more effectively. That's what this chapter is about—using your stress-busting tools (see Chapter 4) to improve your school experience and get more out of it. We don't guarantee that you'll start loving every moment of school, but you *can* learn to stress less.

THINK ABOUT IT: What would you do to make your school a less stressful place? Let your imagination take off (for example, all students get electric scooters to go from class to class). Now think about some realistic changes that would truly add to your enjoyment of school. Who might you share some of these ideas with? Could you talk to teachers, student council members, or your principal? Or write an editorial for your school newspaper?

Courage and your comfort zone

Your comfort zone is the sense of security you have when you know your way around a situation. Whenever you're forced to move out of your comfort zone, that messes with your equilibrium, making you feel off-balance. But being out of your comfort zone isn't always a bad thing. At times, you have to take on new challenges and push yourself, even if you feel uneasy. If you never had to work hard or take any risks, you might feel safe but life would be boring, wouldn't it?

At school, you may be very *uncomfortable* taking a test, speaking in front of your class, or talking about a problem with a teacher. If you were afraid of skydiving, it wouldn't matter because you don't actually *have* to do it. But if you're out of your comfort zone and completely stressed at school, then it's going to take clear thinking and courage to face the challenges.

Having realistic expectations

Do you think you've got to ace every test or always produce perfect work? Part of that pressure may be your temperament, a natural tendency to have high expectations and be detail-oriented and precise. Or, maybe a parent constantly pushes you to be number one and you're anxious that you don't measure up. Wanting to succeed or do your best isn't the same as aiming for perfection. No one is perfect, and trying to live up to an impossible standard can be a huge source of stress. Do you:

- think that nothing you do or have is good enough?
- constantly tell others how they can improve themselves or their work?
- dread failure and/or expect it?
- worry about beginning and/or completing tasks?
- find it hard (if not impossible) to accept a compliment?
- have trouble relaxing?
- believe that if you ever do something "exactly right," you'll be a better, happier person?
- think that people at home will love you only if you're perfect?

If you answered yes to many of these questions, you're too hard on yourself. Pressuring yourself to be superhuman demands that you achieve the impossible, which can affect your health, your self-esteem, and your relationships. Why not consciously choose to flex those impossible standards? (*Flexing* is tool #3.)

You can still have *high* standards and do your best to succeed, but you don't have to carry the added burden of perfection on your shoulders. Tell yourself—and any of the adults who push you— that you're working on having more realistic expectations of your- self. Ask for their support. Set reasonable goals and take your time enjoying the process of going after them. Life isn't a race that you have to win.

WRITE ABOUT IT: Who do you know who tries to do every- thing perfectly? How much enjoyment does that person seem to get out of life? That's a good indication of how well-balanced he or she might be. In your journal, write some advice you might give this person.

On the other hand, maybe your problem is of a different nature: You may be struggling in school as a result of having a learning difference that you're unaware of. Maybe the results from some educational testing would be really helpful for you, your teachers, and your parents to know about. Maybe you're falling behind on your subjects or you're bored. Do you know what your learning style is (visual, auditory, kinesthetic, verbal, etc.) and the specific strategies that go with that style that would make school work easier for you? Talking to a school counselor about this might be an important step. Maybe you don't have much support at home, and you feel like nothing you do at school matters. It does! Or, maybe you're helping your family pay the bills by working a part-time job in addition to being a student, and you're finding it difficult to balance all that you need to do.

Whatever the situation may be, it's stressful. At times, you may feel too overwhelmed to get back on track. But if you struggle through school without ever raising your hand or speaking up about what's going on with you, you're *choosing* to stay silent. Remember, you always have choices—and those choices matter. They matter to you now, and they have a huge impact on your future. Even if you're having a lot of difficulties in school, you can get help and support. But the first step is yours to take.

If you're not doing well in certain classes, talk to your teachers about your areas of difficulty. Do you need to go back and relearn some basic math skills so you can understand algebra? Do you need a tutor who can help you polish your reading skills? Do you struggle with writing, and if so, can you get extra support in classes that include a lot of essays and papers? Is your schedule too heavy? Are your commitments to your after-school job, sports, or other activities making it hard for you to stay on top of your assignments? Your teachers are supposed to be there to help you succeed, not to make your life more difficult. But they need to hear from *you* about what's making school such a challenge, and they'd probably welcome the chance to help you improve your situation.

You have other resources too, including all sorts of adults who care about you: parents or relatives, your school counselor, or your principal. Talk to them about your challenges; ask for their guidance. Many students need extra support in high school, so you're not alone. Getting a tutor or joining a study group could help you catch up and build your skills. You *deserve* a good education, and you have the right to pursue one.

School: Your Incredible Balancing Act (8 Tips for Coping)

1. **Take good class notes:** This is one of those staple skills you need. If your handwriting is a mess or you type faster than you write, look into the option of either tape recording lectures or using a laptop. Keep notes from each class in separate notebooks or binders to stay organized. Missed a class? Get the notes from a friend as soon as you can. Review your notes often—not just before tests.

2. **Set up a quiet workspace:** At home, a well-lit, organized desk will help you work more calmly and efficiently.

3. **Use a calendar or a day planner:** Write down every assignment and scheduled activity. Check your calendar on Mondays (for the weeklong view), as well as daily to make sure you're in the right place when you need to be and are getting your work done.

4. **Create a daily homework schedule:** Knowing, for example, that 7 to 9 p.m. is homework time (no phone calls or IMs) will help you stay on top of your work.

5. **Use your time wisely:** Got a test tomorrow, and you're committed to a game until evening? Use your lunch or free period to get a jump on your studying. Keep your notes and textbooks handy on the bus or wherever, so you can look at them during downtime.

6. **Be realistic:** You're a full-time student: Don't box yourself into a stress corner by overscheduling. If you're having trouble keeping up in school, you may have to give up at least one extracurricular activity or cut back on your hours at your after-school job.

7. **Stay focused:** If you start your homework, try to finish it. Short breaks are healthy and important, but say "no thanks for now" to distractions that take you off task for too long.

8. **Schedule time off:** You need time to yourself and to relax with friends. Having some fun every day will help you stay balanced.

Handling your fears

When you think of a "performance," you probably picture some kind of entertainment on a stage. But in school, you're often required to perform on a daily basis (think pop quizzes, tests, oral presentations). You may have teachers who expect a lot of class participation or who call on you even if your hand isn't raised. That's a lot of pressure from the outside—and, inside, you may often feel like you're tied up in knots.

Once you learn to be afraid of something, like tests, your brain gets programmed to link that thing with fear and stress. In this panicky state, you can't think as clearly, which makes it a whole lot harder to perform under pressure. Same goes for oral reports or speeches. You may get so scared and freaked out about public speaking that you can barely remember a word you're supposed to say.

FACT!

For most people, the fear of public speaking ranks #1. In other words, most of us are more scared of standing up in front of a crowd than we are of death or disease.

TALK ABOUT IT: Talk with someone you know who seems comfortable with performing in front of people (for example, a friend or an adult who plays in a band). Ask that person if he or she ever gets stage fright or has tips on dealing with it.

Facing these fears is a step in the right direction, but how can you do this when you feel too scared to move? Depending on how big your fears are, you may need adult help to work through some of them. Your school counselor, for example, may be able to help you with test anxiety. You could talk to your teacher about the difficulties you have with oral presentations and ask for some tips on getting ready beforehand. Teachers can be good resources because they're used to talking in front of a group every day. It also helps to use the get-back-in-balance tool kit, especially tool #1, *breathing.* Taking re-centering breaths before, during, and after a test or speech can help you calm down and clear your head. You can read more about the breathing tool on page 54.

FACT!
Drinking soda or coffee before a test or an oral report will only make you more nervous. Stick with water, which will help you stay hydrated and balanced.

Still, nothing fights performance anxiety better than being prepared. Here are a few tips for getting ready:

- Give yourself adequate time to review the material you'll be tested on or to rehearse your report.
- Ask friends or family members to quiz you on what you know or to be an audience for your speech.
- Practice in front of the mirror as much as you need to. Rehearse during your spare moments, like when you're on the bus or in the shower.
- If your worries start to run wild, harness that energy for *preparation* instead. Stay focused so you don't have time to let your fears take over.

Meanwhile, stay in good shape physically and mentally by eating right, exercising, and getting the sleep you need (for more tips, see Chapter 3). You'll be sharper if you take care of those basics. Pulling all-nighters in the days leading up to a test or report is never a good idea. Sleep deprivation is a stressor—so is hunger. Stay balanced by making sure you feel your best from head to toe.

English was **EDUARDO'S** second language, and he spoke it very well. When he was with his friends and he sometimes messed up his words, it was no big deal; but in class, Eduardo felt embarrassed about saying the wrong thing. To him, being called on by his teacher was like being in the spotlight, which he hated. He preferred a backstage role, like when he created digital sound effects and ran the computer audio files during play performances. He knew he didn't ever want to be onstage like some of his friends. He wondered why his teachers didn't seem to understand that and kept calling on him in class.

Lately, it had gotten to the point where Eduardo felt sweaty and sort of sick in class. He constantly worried about being called on, and he never raised his hand. Eduardo was confident about his written work, and he brought home A's and B's, but some of his teachers based a lot of the grades they gave on class participation.

After class one day, Eduardo's history teacher asked him to stay and talk. "You've done well on all the quizzes we've had so far," she said, "and I think you know the material, but you don't seem to speak up much in class, Eduardo. I'd love to hear your opinion once in a while."

Eduardo didn't want to tell her about how uncomfortable he felt talking in front of the other students. Instead, he nodded his head and promised to raise his hand more often.

Later, after thinking some more about the situation, Eduardo remembered what his grandmother once told him: that everyone has to push beyond their comfort zone sometimes. He decided to call her after school to see if she had any advice. She asked him something unexpected: "What's the worst that might happen if you were to give an answer and it was wrong, or if you were to make a mistake with your English?"

"I don't know," Eduardo said. "I guess I'd feel like a fool."

"Is that the worst that could happen?" she asked.

"Well, maybe people would laugh or make fun of me," he added.

"Is that the worst then? Being made fun of? It wouldn't feel good, but you'd be able to handle that, Eduardo," his grandmother reminded him.

"Yeah, I guess I could." After he hung up, Eduardo realized that he'd been worried for a long time over something that really might not be as bad as he thought.

The next day in history, he got up his courage and raised his hand the first time his teacher asked a question. She called on him, and he took a deep breath and answered. His teacher said, "Right," and smiled. Eduardo felt relieved. Then he realized he'd been spending most of every class trying to hide so his teacher wouldn't call on him. It felt much better to be able to look at his teacher while she talked. Eduardo promised himself to remember that.

Many of us are afraid of looking foolish in front of others, making mistakes, or failing. And sometimes the fear becomes so strong that it feels easier to run away than to deal with whatever is scaring us.

Pushing yourself out of your comfort zone and facing a fear takes courage. You might ask yourself, "What's the worst that could happen?" Let your imagination create the worst-case scenario and what you might do. You can even have some fun with this (laughter is a de-stressor). In Eduardo's case, he might write down, "If I give a wrong answer in class, it will make front-page headlines around the world. My friends will never speak to me again. I'll be kicked out of class and will never graduate from high school." Obviously, none of these outcomes is likely. Imagining the worst can help you see that the situation may not be as scary as it seems.

Eduardo used tool #2, *thinking.* Instead of ignoring his fear and his teacher's request for him to speak up more, Eduardo went to his grandmother and asked her for advice. After thinking over her words, Eduardo made a choice the next day to behave differently in class (tool #4, *choosing*). His choice paid off.

One other skill you can use to boost your confidence is *visualization,* or mental imagery. All sorts of performers—athletes, musicians, actors—have used this technique to calm their nerves and envision their success before any type of performance. For example, pro athletes visualize themselves scoring goals, hitting homeruns, or achieving their most difficult moves. Visualization is a great stress reliever and fear reducer because it helps you *focus on the positive.* While visualizing, you can imagine yourself filling in the correct answers on a test, giving a great speech, or successfully meeting any challenge you may have in school. This confidence-building technique, plus your good preparation, will help you succeed.

To make the most of visualization, take several re-centering breaths first. And to help yourself relax, lie down on the floor or on your bed and perform the following sequence of tightening and releasing your muscles:

- Start at your head. Tense the muscles in your forehead and jaw, holding for a count of five. Breathe in and, as you exhale, let those muscles relax.

- Move to your shoulders. Squeeze your shoulder blades together and tighten your chest muscles. Hold again for a count of five as you breathe in; as you breathe out, relax the muscles.

- Relax your arms. First tighten them by clenching your fists, locking your elbows, and pushing your arms toward the floor. Count to five as you hold them in this position. Take a deep breath, let it out, and release the tension in your arms and hands.

- Move the focus to your stomach. Clench your abdominal muscles and tighten your rear end. Hold this position, count to five, inhale; as you exhale, relax your muscles.

- Relax your legs. Tighten these muscles by flexing your thighs and pushing your knees and heels down. Breathe and release, as you've been doing. Feel your legs and feet go limp.

➤ Once you feel calmer and more relaxed, close your eyes and create a vivid mental picture of yourself facing the task ahead of you. Imagine each move you make in detail. So, if your challenge is a biology test, see yourself sitting at your desk, looking at the first question, and knowing the answer. Picture yourself as confident, secure. You read the next question, and you answer it easily; you keep going, making your way through each page of the test until you finish.

➤ As the scene unfolds in your mind, focus on positive emotions. Let yourself feel happy, proud, and self-assured. Allow your worries to fade away. Your brain and body will remember this peaceful, relaxed state, and that will help increase your confidence when you face the *real* challenge.

➤ Visualize a few times per day before any test or performance. Get comfortable with the technique and use it whenever needed.

Surviving the social scene

For some people, fitting in socially at school doesn't seem to be an issue. They have a group they feel comfortable in or close friends to hang out with. But for others, the question "Where do I fit in?" causes a lot of stress. Sometimes, the stress lasts for months or even an entire school year (or longer). Because long-term stress not only affects your success in school but also harms your health, getting a grip on this one is really important.

Have you had problems fitting in or being accepted?

"I really love this girl, and she feels the same. But she's two inches taller than me. Everyone looks at us weird at school. We also get picked on, not just looked at strange."
—Byron, 14

"I'm deaf in one ear, and my speech isn't that clear. Everywhere I go, people make fun of me. I feel sad and left out. I also feel very angry and just want friends. I try to fit in, but it is hard to join in when no one wants you around. This seems to be a problem that never goes away."
—Paul, 11

"I am a virgin and proud of it too. There are not a lot of virgins my age near here. I don't have a boyfriend because of this."
—Teresa, 14

"All of my friends are telling me that I should break up with my girlfriend. It's really annoying because I like her a lot. It's kind of like they are trying to control my life or that I have to live up to their expectations."
—Ethan, 15

"When I wasn't accepted into a 'group,' I tried to figure out why. I realized that no matter how hard it would be to be alone, I would never change to fit their status. The only way to have good friends that last forever is to find ones you don't have to change for, and I am better because of it."
—Renata, 14

Have you been teased and, if so, what was it like?

"When I started school, kids would tease me about acting different. I kind of had an idea that I was gay, but I didn't know what the terminology was at the time."
—Fredo, 18

"I've been teased about the fact that I like role-playing games, get the best marks in school, have very few friends, don't dress like everyone else, don't like the same music as everyone else, and more!"
—Matt, 16

"I learned to ignore the taunts and just be myself."
—Gordy, 14

"I just acted like the people who teased me weren't there. It didn't really bother me enough to be upset about it privately. I guess at the beginning of the year, I got upset about it. I realized they were not going to stop, so I learned to live with it."
—Cody, 15

"I was extremely bitter. But I take more pride and get more happiness from the fact that by simply existing and going about my days as I normally would, the people who dislike me and tease me are driven insane. I think that's one of the biggest rewards possible."
—Jon, 16

"The kids at my school tease others 'cause it attracts attention to themselves. Like 'Hey look at me, I can be mean and immature!'"
—Calvin, 13

"I was the butt of a lot of jokes in sixth grade. When someone cracked a 'joke' that I just could not tolerate, I snapped. I reacted, and I just amused them further. All I could do afterward was just cry."
—Haley, 13

Teasing. Peer pressure. Cliques. Bullying. Harassment. Any of these triggers can push your hot buttons, throw you out of your comfort zone, and launch you right into a stress response. Sometimes, you may be the brunt of teasing or insults—but at other times, you may be the one who hurts someone else. Often, you'll be a witness, silent or not, to what happens to others.

Depending on where you live and what your school is like, social pressures like these may be extreme or just bothersome. And depending on your own temperament and feelings about fitting in, you may believe that it's important for you to be part of the "popular" group, to be liked by a wide variety of people from many groups, or to be different from everyone else. Do you often feel like you're being pushed and pulled in different directions? Many teens do. But you're not made of rubber, and you can only stretch so far before you snap.

 THINK ABOUT IT: Have you ever been in a situation where you tried to change something about yourself so that other people might like you? How did you feel when making that change and afterward? Have you ever watched a friend try to turn into a completely different type of person just to be accepted? What was that like for you? What, if anything, changed in your relationship with that friend?

You can't please all of the people all of the time. Besides, if pleasing others means being at war with yourself, you'll never win. You shouldn't have to change who you are to be "popular" or pretend to be someone you're not to fit into a group. Acceptance isn't worth such a high price. If you're true to yourself, you may not have all the friends in the world, but you'll be more at peace with yourself—and that's a very strong and secure place to be.

What does being true to yourself really mean? That you value your unique qualities, strengths, and talents. That you know your own temperament. That you have a set of values you live by. Self-acceptance is a feeling that you like who you are but realize there's always room for a little improvement (no one's perfect). This isn't some ego trip—it's okay to think highly of yourself and look out for your own best interests. The more self-accepting you are, the less stressed you may be. Why? Because having an inner sense that you matter can help guide you in making choices that are right for you. You'll be stronger when facing the pressures of life—and better able to bounce back when those pressures bring you down.

Is it realistic to expect every single person at school to accept you for who you are and treat you with total respect? In a perfect world, yes. In the real world of life at your school, probably not. But that doesn't mean you have to put up with people teasing you or treating you like you're invisible. Like we always say, you've got choices. You can choose to believe people's criticisms or harsh comments—or you can ignore them and continue believing in yourself. You can choose to get stressed out when other people are mean—or you can hold your head high and walk away. Your choices help to define you. Let your choices reflect your true self.

Getting a sense of perspective about the social scene at your school may help too. Know that what goes on in the hallways of many middle and high schools isn't much like the wider world. In a few years, you'll be out of there and you'll have college or a job to look forward to. Even if you stay in your home community, you'll probably see the people in your class eventually outgrowing

their current cliques or roles. If you have at least one close friend you can always trust and count on, that may be all you need.

TALK ABOUT IT: Ask some of the adults in your family what it was like for them in high school. Were there cliques? How about labels like "geek" or "jock"? How did the students treat each other? Has one of your parents or grandparents gone back to any high school reunions, and if so, what was that like? How had people changed? What was the most *surprising* change?

If the social problems you face at school are more serious than what's been described here, you still have choices. Being harassed or bullied, for example, can make school a nightmare, but the law is on *your* side. You have the legal right to receive an education and to feel safe at school. If you're being insulted or assaulted day after day, you don't have to put up with it. Or, if you're a witness when someone else is verbally or physically harassed, you can do something about that too. Report the incidents to your teachers and your principal. Let the adults at home know what you've experienced or witnessed, and see what they can do to help. Ask your friends to stand by you and to report what they've seen as well. Change can start with one or two individuals who have the courage to step forward and speak up.

By now, you know that you always have options for de-stressing or defusing tough situations, and this is true everywhere: at school, at home, and in your community.

You're in charge of what you do and say, and of how you react to stressful people or events. You can use your stress-busting tools whenever needed and continue building a network of friends and adults who support you. All of these efforts will help you face life's challenges with greater courage. You'll be stronger, more stress resistant, and better able to keep forging your own path.

PART
3

Taking Care
of Yourself
(Because You're Worth It)

dating   jobs   family   pressure
cliques   homework   identity   tests
bullying   friends

9

Take Time to Relax

Becoming a more balanced person requires conscious choices about how you spend your free time. Yes, we know you're very busy, but everyone has *some* free time. There are fun things you can do every day to get your mind off your problems, to manage stress, and to enjoy life. Find what you like and consciously choose to make the time to do it on a regular basis—that's the key.

When people are stressed, they tend to spend a lot of time in the stress traps (avoiding stuff, procrastinating, obsessing, worrying). Guess what? The traps make people feel . . . trapped. To avoid this, you can trade some of the time you spend in the traps for time doing things you enjoy. Having positive activities in your life is a guaranteed de-stressor.

Not sure what kind of activities would be good stress busters? That's what this chapter is for.

FACT!

You don't have to wait until you're anxious to do something relaxing. Re-centering is a way to relax, and you can do it anytime. In fact, if you incorporate calming activities into your day-to-day life, you'll probably find yourself feeling more balanced and centered most of the time.

Creativity soothes

Everyone has the ability to come up with ideas. That's where creativity starts—with an idea and a desire to explore it. When you create, you bring something new into the world using your imagination and your expressive abilities. The creative process lets you go deep inside yourself, and the results are often surprising. Not knowing where you'll end up is part of the fun.

You don't have to be a great artist or poet to be creative. You just need to be willing to try. You can create things that are meant for *your* eyes and ears only. Or you can decide to share this part of yourself with others—it's completely up to you. If what you create doesn't turn out the way you envisioned, don't stress about it. The creative experience is about the process, not the product. If you've got that down, then the activity itself will help bring more balance into your life.

Journal. If you haven't already started keeping a journal, how about starting now? Pick a notebook or a blank book, or use a sketchbook or even a computer. Your private journal can serve as a place to sort out your thoughts and feelings, as well as to vent or rant. Ask yourself questions about your experiences, dreams, and wishes for the future. Write about interesting things you've observed in others (or yourself) during the course of a day. When you keep a journal, it's amazing to go back and reread it to see the changes in your worldview or mood from week to week, month to month, or even year to year.

Write. Some people find that writing stories is a creative way to work out all kinds of stressful life situations. In fiction, the author is the boss. You can send your characters down difficult roads and be 100 percent in charge of their motivations, obstacles, choices, consequences, and reactions. Talk about power! Nonfiction writing can also open up your mind beyond the immediate world you see every day. For example, doing one oral history of an aunt, an uncle, or a grandparent might reveal family stories that broaden your understanding of your parents' lives. Other nonfiction writing includes essays, zines, or blogs. Or what about poetry? Poetry can be a fun challenge because it helps you explore your ideas and emotions in few words. Your poems don't need to rhyme or have perfect meter—anything goes.

Play an instrument. Playing an instrument is a terrific way to lower the stress of everyday life. You can express all kinds of feelings, moods, and thoughts without words. If you don't play, then just listen to music. Borrow CDs from the library or from friends, with a goal of trying forms of music you rarely listen to. Classical, jazz, blues, opera, bluegrass—all can stretch your mind and surprise you.

Jam. You don't have to have a band with a name, an audience, or gigs in order to play music with friends in a spontaneous way. Maybe you like to jam in someone's garage. When two or three people get together and play for an hour or two, it can take you to surprising places while reducing stress. When jamming with others, you get to hear what your friends have to "say" without words, and they hear you too. Plus, you're putting music into the world—always a good thing.

Sing. Sing whenever and wherever—just use your voice, whether you think it sounds good or not. When you sing, you temporarily step into another world and leave stress behind. Try singing in a chorus, a choir, a band, or in the shower, car, or kitchen. If you've never experienced karaoke, give it a try. If you can't stand your voice and singing is out of the question, just lip sync.

Draw/paint. Did you give up drawing or painting at some point, convinced you weren't any good? No one has to see your work (and it may be a lot better than you think, anyway). Get some watercolors and work on a landscape or something totally abstract. Draw with pencils, ink, charcoal, or pastels. Don't have a lot of money for art materials? Just go outside with paper and a pencil and sketch the trees, look in the mirror to create a self-portrait, or create your own black-and-white comic. Don't say you can't draw a straight line—art isn't about straight lines! If you truly don't want to draw or paint, how about making a collage with found objects, like branches, candy wrappers, and/or bottle caps?

Work with your hands. There are other ways to use your hands besides drawing and painting: How about sewing, knitting, crocheting, beading, sculpting, or making pottery? These activities can be relaxing and productive at the same time—and they take your mind off stress and problems.

Perform. Love that audience waiting for the curtain to rise? Then performing might be your thing. What do you like to do? Dance, act, sing, play an instrument? You can join the chorus at school, sign up for dance classes, try out for plays, start a band, or audition for the school orchestra. All of these activities involve discipline, practice, and discovery. Working with others brings an added dimension of challenge and fun.

Document your life (and the lives of others). Whether you take photos, make a video, or create a scrapbook, visually documenting your own experience or that of others can be inspiring. Again, you're taking time you might otherwise spend worrying and using that energy positively. You get the chance to share your point of view and talents and, in the process, regain a sense of balance.

Do puzzles. For some people, there's hardly anything more satisfying than putting in the last piece of a huge jigsaw puzzle or figuring out the key word in that final corner of a crossword puzzle. For others, it's about the process more than the solution. What kind of puzzles do you like? Brainteasers? Word scrambles? Acrostics? How about 3-D jigsaw puzzles or Rubik's Cube? Working on solutions to these problems gets your brain going in new directions.

Cook/bake. Never thought of cooking as creative? It can be, if you do more than nuke some macaroni and cheese. Find a recipe for a dish that you think you'd love (the Internet has thousands of cooking sites), get the ingredients together, and see what kind of culinary wizard you may be. Another option is to try baking—anything from bread to pie to cookies. Kneading dough can be wonderfully therapeutic; the aromas that fill the kitchen will tempt your senses too. And the results of your efforts? Delicious, or at least interesting. If you make enough food to share, you're doing something nice for your family and friends.

Garden. Planting, weeding, watering, and tending flowers and/or vegetables will connect you to the earth and help you feel centered. If you don't have a yard, you can still plant in containers on a front step. You can connect with growing things even if you only have a small plant on your windowsill. As an alternative, some cities have community gardens, places where urban gardeners can come together, get their hands dirty, and de-stress.

Build. You can build anything that captures your interest: a birdhouse, a piece of furniture, or a model airplane, ship, or car. Pounding with a hammer relieves stress. And the precision of working with small-scale models requires concentration—which means you're not thinking about any problems other than the ones the model itself might present.

Fix stuff. Maybe you're a great problem-solver who also loves to work with your hands. If so, fixing things at home might be a good way for you to express your creativity and de-stress. And if, for example, you manage to repair the annoying kitchen drawer that always gets stuck, you'll be helping your family lower *their* stress levels as well.

Short breaks and great escapes

Everyone needs a break at times. In fact, knowing when you need one and then taking it is a great way to stay in balance. When you're working hard on a school project or you're involved in an intense conversation, it can feel good to get away from it for a while and try something different. After re-energizing and clearing your head, you'll be better able to complete what you were doing.

One thing about breaks—they need a clear ending point. Go ahead and play a video game, but don't get so lost in it that you blow off your homework or time with friends. Same goes for TV and teen magazines: Check them out only if they interest you and in short doses. Make sure they relax you or spark your creativity. If TV, magazines, and other media tend to stress you out more, then minimize the time you spend with them.

Here are some things teens told us they like to do when they're in break mode:

Listen to music. Music can energize or calm you, depending on what kind it is and how you react to it. Listen to all your old favorites and find ways to expose yourself to new music too. You can borrow CDs from friends, family members, or the library; you can try out new radio stations locally or online. Why not find your own "pump-me-up" theme song that you love, and then play it whenever you need a boost?

Take a hot bath or shower. There's nothing as relaxing as a long, hot bath or shower for soaking away your stress. Loosen your muscles and breathe in the steam. If you're into it, add some bubble bath or light some candles.

Talk to friends. Whether you talk face to face, or chat on the phone or online, talking to friends is a super stress reliever. Your friends probably know all the right ways to make you laugh, and they may even be good problem-solvers and advice-givers. Next time you need a break, find one of your friends and take a break together.

Read for pleasure. Read everything from great novels to comic books. Try essays, newspapers, news magazines, graphic novels, or books about history, science, or art. Visit Web sites. Go to the library. Reread old stories you've always loved. Reading can be the perfect getaway, especially if you have a special place you enjoy, like a cozy corner of the couch, a park bench, or your bed.

Watch movies or TV. Want an easy break? Watch a favorite TV show or ask your family to take you to the movies. It's fun to get lost in the story or try to guess the plot twists. And if you watch the show or movie with other people, you've got something fun to talk about afterward (a nice way to get your mind off your troubles).

Play computer or video games. Sure, these can be distracting and violent and all the other negative things you might have heard about gaming. But sometimes, computer/video games are just a way to have fun. Keep your game breaks short so you can get back to real life.

Clean. (No, this is a misprint!) Some people find cleaning to be relaxing. If you're one of them, you know the positive feelings that something as simple as cleaning off your desk can inspire. Try straightening up your closet, reorganizing a drawer, or making your bed. Whatever works!

Shop. Even if you don't have a lot of money or a list of things to buy, you may enjoy window-shopping. It can be fun to try on clothes, check out new books and music, stop at the arcade, and visit with friends.

Experience the great outdoors. Getting some fresh air and sunshine can do wonders. It sure beats sitting inside all day. Try to get outside as often as you can, no matter what the weather. Walk the dog on a rainy afternoon. Enjoy the wind or heat or cold. Afterward, come in for a hot (or chilled) drink to refresh yourself.

Enjoy nature. Head to a nearby park and take in the view. Notice the trees, bushes, flowers, anthills, people, pets, sky, and other sights. Find a swing. Try out the slide and jungle gym—you're not too old for this stuff. Look at your surroundings with fresh eyes and have some fun.

Walk, jog, run. Human beings are built for movement, and that's why most of us get crabby when we've been sitting around all day. You have to sit in school and on the bus, and you often have to come home and sit some more to do your homework. In between all that sitting, be sure you're getting enough exercise (you can read more about that in Chapter 3). Take walks or go out for a run. Put on your in-line skates or hop on your skateboard. When you have more time, like on weekends, go for long hikes with your friends and family in the woods, on local trails, or around town.

Laugh—You'll Feel Better

Experts say that laughter reduces stress hormones, triggers the release of endorphins, and produces a general sense of well-being. How can you get more laughter in your life? By reading the comics, learning new jokes, watching funny sitcoms or a comedy channel, checking out the humor section of your local bookstore, and even observing little kids and pets (who do a lot of funny things without realizing it). When you laugh, you feel less tense and a whole lot happier. And because laughter is contagious, you can "infect" all your friends and help them de-stress as well.

Helping others helps you too!

When we're stressed, many of us become self-absorbed, thinking only about our problems and how we feel about them. We worry, we blame ourselves or everyone else, and we become more stressed.

The teens who answered our survey often said that when they're stressed they feel "helpless," "powerless," and "like a failure." That's what stress does—it robs us of feeling like we're confident and in control of our own lives. We go into survival mode, wanting to fight, run, or hide. Throughout this book, you're learning ways to outsmart that stress response and bring more balance into your life. Reaching out to help others is one of those ways.

When you volunteer your time to help a cause you care about, you start to see yourself as someone who can get things done and make others feel better. And that's empowering. Helping others also gets you back in balance because you start to see that you're not alone. You're part of a community that includes a whole lot of people who are willing to support each other. When you help out, you make connections. You can give and get support when you need it.

Volunteering also provides a healthy sense of perspective. This is a *huge* world we live in, one filled with all sorts of needs and challenges. You can help fill those needs—and you can rise to those challenges. Think about who or what you might want to help: Children? Other teens? Senior citizens? People in disadvantaged circumstances? People with disabilities? Animals? Wildlife? The environment? The arts? The moment you feel inspired, take one step toward connecting with others as a volunteer. Here are some ways to do this:

Join a club at school. See if your school has a service club you can become a part of. It's more fun to volunteer with other people, and you may feel empowered when you get things done as a group.

Look for local opportunities. Check out your community newspaper or magazine for volunteering positions. Look at the bulletin boards at your community center, library, YMCA, or YWCA. See if you can walk dogs or help clean cages at your local Humane Society. Visit a retirement center to ask if they're looking for helpers. You can also go to Volunteer Match (www.volunteermatch.org); enter your postal code and press "Search" to get a list of volunteer opportunities in your area.

Volunteer through your place of worship. A faith community is a natural place for serving others. Find out what your place of worship does to help people in your community, and then get involved.

Be a mentor. Have you ever thought of mentoring a younger child? Many kids need a teen to look up to and learn from. As a mentor, you could help a child learn to read, have more confidence, or gain more social skills. Look into mentoring experiences through your school, community center, or place of worship.

Make donations. You could gather used clothing or household items for a charity. You could donate canned goods to a food shelf or homeless shelter. Or you could give a portion of your allowance or paycheck to a worthy cause. Maybe you could do all three?

Getting quiet and centered

Most likely, your mind is buzzing all day long. Thoughts pop in and out: "I'm late for science," "Did she just look at me weird?" "I have gym today," "What's up with Dad?" "Not another test!" "I hope he asks me out," "Did I bring my cleats?" "I'm so hungry . . ." And that's on a *good* day. On a day when you're stressed, you might feel like a deer in the headlights. And after *days and days* of being stressed? Well, it's not a pretty picture.

Constant stress is like a toxin. Fortunately, there's a powerful antidote. That is, getting quiet and centered to clear your mind, calm your body, and feed your soul. So, how do you achieve this particular state of being? By taking time to just *be.* Sound weird?

Think about it: How often do you feel like you're *in the moment,* or in the *here and now?* Too often, as human beings, we're thinking about what we have to do next, what we haven't gotten done, or what we did but wished we hadn't. We forget to stop, breathe, and enjoy life.

You don't have to fill every waking hour with things that keep you busy and require a lot of physical and mental energy. In fact, you'll be a lot happier and healthier if you don't. Sometimes, you need to take time out to enjoy the quiet—and to get quiet inside. That means temporarily pulling the plug on all the technology that may distract you: TV, computer, CD player, phone, whatever. Go to a peaceful place indoors or outdoors. Take time to just be present in the moment. Here are some ideas:

Be alone. Make a conscious choice to enjoy your own company on a regular basis. It's great to have family and friends in your life, but you still need some alone time to experience a stronger sense of who you are and what's important to you. Can you find a quiet place to go to when you want to be alone? Anywhere will work, even a closet.

Explore. Step outside your front door and observe your surroundings, letting whatever catches your eye determine what you'll explore. You may think you know your neighborhood inside and out because you've walked or driven down a certain street hundreds of times. But even the same old sights might surprise you, if you consciously choose to pay attention to details. Allow yourself to really see what's in front of you: the veins on a leaf, the shadows on the sidewalk, the movement of the clouds. Being mindful of your surroundings helps you tune in to the world—and yourself—in new ways.

Daydream. Do you ever feel guilty about daydreaming? Maybe you've been told by adults to stop daydreaming and start paying more attention. But daydreaming isn't a total waste of time. It's a way to exercise your imagination, get lost in your own creative musings, and figure out what you wish for in life. That can be time well spent.

Challenge yourself (in unusual ways). To become more aware and less automatic in the way you live moment to moment, give yourself an unusual daily challenge. For example, you might write with your opposite hand, or communicate without words for a designated period of time. This forces you to pay attention to what you're doing in new ways and to tune out some of your own mental noise.

Belly breathing and meditation

In Chapter 4, you learned about re-centering breaths and how they can help you control your stress response. Another kind of conscious breathing is *deep belly breathing.* Because it takes more time than a re-centering breath, belly breathing isn't meant for on-the-spot stress relief. Rather, it's like a warm bath for your spirit and should be practiced when you've got the time to learn how it works and to make the most of it.

When combined with meditation, deep breathing can lead you to a greater sense of calm and balance. Maybe you think of meditation as a weird new-age thing or a celebrity trend. Actually, people have been meditating for thousands of years, and experts have proven that it reduces stress and promotes a sense of well-being. Why does it work? Because it helps slow your breathing and pulse, it enhances communication between the left- and right-hand sides of the brain, and it boosts your physical energy (among other benefits). But you can't just meditate/breathe deeply once and expect your life to change. You have to do it for a certain amount of time every day (or nearly every day) to reap the benefits.

Here's how, step by step:

1. Find a quiet place. Go where you can be alone and won't get interrupted. Some people like to be in nature, while others prefer an indoor environment. See what works for you. Remind your family that you need some privacy.

2. Get into a comfortable position. You can lie down on the floor, sit on the floor with your back to a wall and your legs straight out in front of you (or cross-legged), or sit on a straight-backed chair with your feet flat on the floor. Find a position that you'll be comfortable in for at least 15 minutes.

3. Rest your hands and eyes. If you're lying down, you can either rest your hands along your sides or place one hand lightly on your chest. If you're seated, you can put your arms and hands in your lap. Another option is to rest your hands on your belly, so you can feel it rising and falling once you start the deep breathing. Now close your eyes.

4. Begin breathing. Inhale through your nose, feeling your chest rise. Exhale through your nose and feel your chest falling. Be sure you're taking slow, deep breaths (as opposed to shallow, quick ones).

5. Now breathe more deeply. This time, when you inhale, consciously try to bring your breath down into your belly. Imagine your belly gently filling up like a balloon. Exhale and see if you can feel your belly growing smaller.

6. Focus on your breath. Stay relaxed and loose (don't tense up). Continue breathing deeply in and out through your nose. If any thoughts come up, let them go and return the focus to your breathing.

7. Add words, if you want to. As you inhale, you might think *in;* as you exhale, think *out.* (Or, think *here* then *now.*)

8. Continue for at least 15 minutes. Focus on your breathing and keep it steady and rhythmic. Stay relaxed. Enjoy!

What do you do to get back in balance?

"Write rap songs."
—Perry, 14

"Sit in a comfortable chair and write in my diary."
—Johanna, 12

"I do Aikido, and they tell you to find your center so I always try that and deep breaths."
—Ross, 12

"I just go draw, paint, or write poetry."
—Marita, 16

"When I'm stressed, I relax by drawing with my left hand (I'm a 'righty'), or I read articles on astronomy."
—David, 13

"Usually, a hot water bottle in bed and a good night's sleep will help me."
—Ursula, 13

"I meditate and stretch."
—Shelley, 18

"I write new stories or add to ones I've started."
—Lily, 12

"Curl up and shut down."
—Walter, 13

"I think about good memories."
—Isabel, 13

"I distract myself by reading, playing video games, listening to music, and doing anything else that can take my mind off of stress."
—Thomas, 13

"I talk to my mother. Expressing my feelings makes me feel as though I have lifted a great burden off my chest."
—Dyanne, 13

"I try to look at the bigger picture and realize that my problem is miniscule to everything else that's going on in the world, good or bad. I take a walk or go for a run to clear my thoughts."
—Michela, 16

"Read an inspirational book or go see a good movie."
—James, 15

"I keep a journal, which helps me to sort out all my feelings."
—Sidra, 18

"I listen to music really loud or play the guitar."
—Joe, 14

"I play with my dog or go shopping."
—Stacey, 17

"If I'm alone, I yell at the top of my lungs."
—Donald, 17

"I usually just go for a walk and try to remember to breathe."
—Monique, 13

10

Get the Help You Need

You've come to the last chapter of this book. We hope you've learned some useful information about what stress is, how it affects your brain and body, and how your own stress response influences the way you think and act. We also hope that you've had some success using the tools to get back in balance when you're dealing with everyday stressors. Maybe you've already started incorporating some of the strategies into your life, which can help you feel less anxious, more positive, and better able to deal with whatever comes up.

But what if no matter what you do, you're still stressed out? Maybe you've reached your limit. Maybe the stressors in your life are much bigger than what most teens have to deal with. Everyday challenges like being too shy to talk to your crush or getting the jitters when you take a math test may seem small compared to what you're living with. Some teens (and you might be one of them) have problems that make their lives feel scary, hopeless, or out of control. These might include:

■ drug or alcohol abuse/addiction

■ an eating disorder

■ an abusive relationship with a family member, adult authority figure, or boyfriend/girlfriend (or memories of past abuse)

■ the death of a loved one

142

- a traumatic event, such as rape or being the victim of an accident or violence

- sexual promiscuity

- identity issues; for example, knowing that you're gay, lesbian, or bisexual, and not feeling supported by family or friends

- suicidal thoughts, attempted suicide, or self-harm (like cutting)

What do you do then? The tools in this book can help you calm down and think more clearly no matter what's causing your stress. But if the issues you're facing are too big to deal with on your own, like the ones mentioned above, then you need additional tools and resources to help you get back in balance.

Take a re-centering breath right here and now. (For how to do that, see page 54.) Remind yourself that *you have options.* No matter how overwhelmed you are or how powerless you feel, there are steps you can take to make things better. Don't lose hope.

But maybe you've convinced yourself that you're alone and no one would understand or care about what you're going through. Perhaps you haven't told anyone what you're dealing with because you think they'd be shocked, angry, or disappointed. Maybe you believe that needing help is a sign of weakness. It's not. It takes a strong person to ask for help.

What can you do if you've reached the limit of what you can handle and you know you need more help than this book can give you? One choice you can make right now is to flex. (That's tool #3; see page 59.) Flexing is about changing your beliefs or outlook. It's not easy to change a way of thinking, to break a habit, or to stop behaving a certain way—it takes time, effort, and support. If you've been telling yourself that no one can help you or no one would listen, then flex by changing that attitude little by little each day. The truth is, you aren't alone, and you don't have to deal with your problems all by yourself. You can choose to reach out and get the help you need. Just realizing you *have* that choice is important.

Even if it's scary at first, talking to the right person will make you feel better. So take a deep breath and deal with whatever resistance you may have. Then open up to someone you trust.

Who do you talk to?

That depends on who's most likely to help you. Talking to your friends can help a lot when you're facing everyday stressors. And having a trusted support network of friends you can count on in good times and bad is a great way to maintain your balance throughout your life (for more on friends, see Chapter 6). When you offer support in return, that's a good feeling—you'll know your friends can trust and rely on you, and that they look to you for advice.

But if you're dealing with heavy-duty stressors, then you need some heavy-duty help. As much as your friends care about you, they probably can't give you the kind of guidance you need. That's why you have to talk to an adult who's professionally trained to work with teens. The professional may be a doctor, psychiatrist, psychologist, therapist, or counselor, depending on what's right for you.

If you haven't yet told the adults in your family about what's going on with you, then it's probably best to do that first. A parent or another adult in your family can then help you get the professional support you may need. If you're scared to talk to a parent or another adult, you can practice saying the words ahead of time. You might start with, "I've got something serious to talk to you about. Is now a good time?" Or, "I really need some help. Can you help me?" Take re-centering breaths as you need to and try to stay calm.

If there's no way you can go to a parent or a family member, don't let that stop you from talking to another trusted adult. Other people to turn to might include an aunt or uncle, a grandparent, a teacher, the school counselor, a religious advisor, an adult friend of your family, or your principal or coach. On pages 151–153, you'll also find a list of hotlines to call for support.

˙What is it like to get professional help?

You deserve to feel happier, stronger, and less stressed than you do—and you can, with the guidance of adults who know how to help. Depending on your situation, you may need to be monitored by a doctor, get some counseling (also called therapy), and/or take medication. Only a trained professional can recommend a treatment plan that's right for you.

But you may be wondering what it's like to seek professional support. For example, many teens have questions about counseling. We can answer some of these questions, but it's best to talk to the adults in your life for further answers.

Basically, counseling is a way for you to learn more about yourself and get help with your problems. Counseling takes place in a private setting with a trained professional (psychologist, therapist, etc.) who helps you sort out your feelings. Some counselors focus on helping teens, while others specialize in family therapy. An adult can help you figure out which kind of counseling may be needed for your situation.

What you say during a counseling session remains confidential between you and your counselor. That level of trust is important because it allows you to talk openly and honestly about what's going on. Counselors are great listeners and can guide you in solving problems. If you're concerned about the adults in your family finding out about what's said in a counseling session, know that what you say has to be kept private. However, this isn't the case if you discuss suicide, injuring yourself, or hurting someone else—or if you talk about someone hurting you. In those circumstances, a counselor is required by law to seek further help for you, even if this means breaking the confidentiality rule.

You might connect well with a counselor, feeling like you can trust him or her and talk about what's going on. On the other hand, you may not feel like you're in sync with the first counselor you see. Give it a chance by going to more than one session before deciding. If you truly think the counselor isn't the right fit for you, try another. Don't give up on what could be a good thing by deciding that counseling was the wrong idea or that all counselors are bad. Like anything new, counseling might feel strange at first—but hang in there.

Counseling is the work of self-discovery: As you learn more about yourself and how you've been shaped by your relationships and environment, you'll gain insight and new tools for dealing with your problems and stress. You and your counselor will most likely set some goals and work together to reach them, using your unique temperament and personal strengths. You might meet once a week or more frequently, with the sessions lasting about an hour. Counseling may continue for weeks, months, or years.

Depending on your family's medical insurance policy, it's possible that many, or some, of the counseling sessions will be partially covered through insurance. But if you discover that counseling isn't an affordable option for you or your family, there are free or low-cost services available in many communities. Start by talking to your principal or school counselor about counseling services that may be available through your school district. Or look in the Yellow Pages for low-cost counseling services. You might also contact a county social worker for more information.

Many young people are reluctant to see a counselor, especially in school, because they worry that other people will find out. But don't let that stop you. Seeing a counselor is your own private business. Counseling can be a positive, supportive, and life-changing experience—an opportunity to get back on a healthier path and regain your balance.

Support groups

In addition to counseling, you may want to explore joining a support group. These groups meet regularly in schools, counseling centers, hospitals, places of worship, and community centers, and they usually focus on specific physical or mental health issues. For example, some support groups help teens to deal with the stress of chemical dependency or of living with an alcoholic or drug-addicted parent. Other groups focus on eating disorders. And still others help people who are dealing with grief and loss.

You can join a support group in your community or online. The main benefit of being in a support group is realizing that other teens are dealing with many of the same issues as you are. Because they've been through similar circumstances or felt the same emotions, these teens will understand where you're coming from and might even inspire you to keep moving in the right direction. You can help them in return by being honest about your feelings and offering your support.

Teens Who've Been There

"I was in drug rehab. My counselor gave me a lot of inspiration and a lot of hope. Basically, she made me feel like I could do whatever I wanted in my life. No one had ever done that for me before."
—Angela, 17

"One thing that really helped me deal with my anxiety was to talk to someone. It could be anyone: parents, a close friend, a counselor. Just getting all your feelings out can take a lot of weight off your shoulders."
—Nick, 15

"I was in an adolescent support group for girls with eating disorders. When I went to the group, I saw all these people who were in recovery and I thought, 'There's hope!' And I realized I didn't have to be in this unhappy, awful life for the rest of my life. All these people were working through it, and there was support here. There were people who would be my friends."
—Vanessa, 14

"It was great to walk into a support group and know that I could talk about whatever I wanted to and leave. It was a helpful environment for me to be in. And some of these people would tell me straight out what was going on because they had been through it."
—Len, 16

When you make the decision to talk to someone, you move in the direction of healing. And that's going to reduce your stress and leave you feeling happier and more in control of your situation. Remember, lots of people care about you—family, friends, relatives, teachers, mentors, and more. If they knew you were hurting, they'd most likely offer you the help you need. Give people a chance to support you.

When you stay connected to others, you do a lot to keep stress at bay. This might require you to flex your attitude about asking for help. Or it may mean that you have to be more open and honest about your problems than you have been in the past. But you can do this. And when you do, you'll be giving yourself exactly what you need to have the kind of life you want and deserve.

dating jobs family pressure

liques homework identity tests

school bullying

friends

A Final Word

The one thing you can count on in life is that things are constantly changing. Sometimes, you get advance warning of the changes so you can prepare yourself. At other times, you may seem to get flattened, full on, without knowing exactly what hit you. In addition to the unexpected bumps and jolts, you'll always be challenged to keep balancing the demands of family, friends, school or work, outside interests, and time just for yourself. But you already *have* what you need to survive and thrive. You've got people close to you who will stand by you. You've got your ability to express yourself so you can work out your feelings. You've also got an inner strength that helps you keep going, even when you feel down and overwhelmed. That strength is at your very core and helps you know what you need to do on your own or with help.

We hope this book has reminded you that being thrown off-balance is an everyday occurrence for all of us. Using what you've learned here can help you get back on your feet and keep moving forward. Here's to keeping your balance!

dating   jobs   family   pressure

cliques   identity   tests
     homework
          school
                    bullying
                         friends

Where to Go for More Info

When the pressure gets to be too much, there are many places to go for help. You can call a helpline if you feel like you need to talk with someone right away. Reading books and browsing Web sites are other great ways to find help and get more information. While not a complete listing, these resources can get you moving toward a life of less stress

Helplines

Al-Anon/Alateen Helpline
1-888-4AL-ANON (1-888-425-2666)
www.al-anon-alateen.org
This organization offers support for families and friends of alcoholics. You can call Monday through Friday from 8 a.m. to 6 p.m. EST to find a chapter near you. Or, look them up online.

ANAD Hotline
(847) 831-3438
www.anad.org
Available Monday through Friday from 9 a.m. to 5 p.m. CST, this number puts you in touch with the National Association of Anorexia Nervosa and Associated Disorders. Call or visit the Web site for information on eating disorders and treatment referrals in your area.

Girls and Boys Town National Hotline

1-800-448-3000

www.girlsandboystown.org

This crisis line is available for teens 24 hours a day, 7 days a week. Professional counselors provide advice on many problems you might face, including family difficulties, depression, and substance abuse.

National Domestic Violence Hotline

1-800-799-SAFE (1-800-799-7233)

www.ndvh.org

This crisis line, available 24/7, has information on over 5,000 nationwide shelters and service providers for those who are victims of domestic violence. Call for information on facilities in your area.

National HIV/AIDS and Sexually Transmitted Disease Hotline

1-800-342-2437

A service of the Centers for Disease Control, this 24-hour hotline provides anonymous, confidential information on HIV, AIDS, and sexually transmitted diseases (STDs). You can also get preventative information and local referrals.

National Hopeline Network Hotline

1-800-SUICIDE (1-800-784-2433)

www.hopeline.com

This free crisis line helps people who are depressed or suicidal— and those who are concerned that someone else might be. The line can connect you to the nearest certified crisis center, where trained counselors are ready to talk 24/7.

National Runaway Switchboard Hotline

1-800-RUNAWAY (1-800-786-2929)

This toll-free, 24-hour hotline provides confidential crisis intervention for a variety of situations, including fights that happen at home, drug and alcohol abuse, and depression. Call for information on counseling services in your area.

RAINN National Sexual Assault Hotline
1-800-656-HOPE (1-800-656-4673)
www.rainn.org
Available 24 hours a day, 7 days a week, this free, confidential counseling hotline is operated by the largest anti-sexual violence organization in the United States, the Rape, Abuse, and Incest National Network. Call or visit the Web site for information about sexual abuse and what you can do if you've been assaulted.

Trevor Helpline
1-866-4-U-TREVOR (1-866-488-7386)
The Trevor Helpline is a free, 24-hour crisis hotline for GLBTQ youth and teens. Call or visit the Web site for information on support groups and resources in your area.

 **Books**

Bringing Up Parents: The Teenager's Handbook by Alex J. Packer (Minneapolis: Free Spirit Publishing, 1993). Full of ideas for resolving conflicts with parents and creating more trust, this book can help you strengthen family relationships and make home a place where you feel less stress.

Dating with Confidence: A Teen's Survival Guide by Jacqueline Jarosz (Avon, MA: Adams Media, 2000). How do you know if you're ready for dating and the dilemmas that come with it? Read this book for the lowdown on dating's potential pitfalls. Included are dating do's and don'ts that can help smooth your way to an enjoyable and relaxing time out.

Don't Sweat the Small Stuff for Teens by Richard Carlson (New York: Hyperion, 2000). A short and simple read, this book covers a variety of topics many teens face daily. You'll find ideas for moving beyond difficult situations and putting smaller stressors in perspective.

Focus on Body Image: How You Feel About How You Look by Maurene J. Hinds (Berkeley Heights, NJ: Enslow Publishers, 2002). Many teens worry a lot about how they look. Full of personal stories from girls and guys who've been there, this book includes information on a variety of body issues.

The "Go Ask Alice" Book of Answers: A Guide to Good Physical, Sexual, and Emotional Health by Columbia University's Health Education Program (New York: Henry Holt and Company, 1998). Based on the popular Web site by the same name, this book offers straightforward, nonjudgmental information on physical, sexual, and emotional health.

HIGHS! Over 150 Ways to Feel Really, REALLY Good Without Alcohol or Other Drugs by Alex J. Packer (Minneapolis: Free Spirit Publishing, 2000). There are many fun and healthy ways to de-stress when you feel twisted up in knots. Find lots of ideas for getting high without chemicals that can harm your body.

Odd Girl Speaks Out: Girls Write About Bullies, Cliques, Popularity, and Jealousy by Rachel Simmons (Orlando, FL: Harcourt Books, 2004). Poems, songs, confessions, and essays from real teen girls who've had problems with other girls—plus advice on resolving conflicts and ending in-fighting.

A Taste Berry Teen's Guide to Managing the Stress and Pressures in Your Life by Bettie Youngs and Jennifer Leigh Youngs (Deerfield Beach, FL: HCI, 2001). A combination of real stories and advice, this book covers different stressful situations you might face—and what you can do when you find yourself in them.

The Teenage Guy's Survival Guide by Jeremy Daldry (New York: Little, Brown and Company, 1999). This book offers the true scoop on growing up as a guy. Find information and advice on surviving school, staying afloat in the social scene, and getting older.

When Nothing Matters Anymore: A Survival Guide for Depressed Teens by Bev Cobain (Minneapolis: Free Spirit Publishing, 1998).

Sometimes stress can take a toll that leaves you feeling depressed. Read this book to learn about symptoms of depression, ways to stay well, and places to go for help if you need it.

Web sites

Big Brothers Big Sisters
www.bbbsa.org
The oldest and largest youth mentoring organization in the United States. Strives to help children reach their potential through professionally supported, one-on-one relationships with measurable impact.

The InSite
www.theinsite.org
Everything from advice on relationships, to a teen soap opera called *The Story,* to an online gallery for teen art and writing. At the heart and soul of The InSite is "Terra," a kind of cyberspace "Dear Abby" who answers thousands of letters (from Hong Kong to Brazil) written by teens just like you.

Mind Your Mind
www.mindyourmind.ca
Taking care of your mind is as important as taking care of your body. This site offers real stress stories from teens, tools for dealing when the pressure is on, and positive, interactive ways to relieve anxiety.

National Eating Disorders Association
www.nationaleatingdisorders.org
Visit this site for information on all forms of eating disorders and treatments—and to get referrals for doctors, counselors, nutritionists, and facilities in your area.

NIDA for Teens
www.teens.drugabuse.gov
Some teens feel so stressed out that they think they have to use alcohol or other drugs to relax. The truth is that these substances

cause your body and mind *more* stress. Visit this site from the National Institute on Drug Abuse for the straight scoop on the science behind how alcohol and other drugs affect your body.

Sex, Etc.

www.sexetc.org

Sponsored by Rutgers University, this site by and for teens is a place to find accurate, up-front information about relationships, health, alcohol and drugs, abuse, violence, body image, and yes, sex.

Teen Growth

www.teengrowth.com

Need help dealing with a problem? You're not alone. This site answers questions from teens on health, tough family topics, surviving school, social life, sports pressures, and more.

Teen Health

www.teenhealth.org

Find articles, answers, and facts on everything related to your health—physical, mental, and sexual. The site also has advice for dealing with tough spots that come up at school, at home, and out with friends.

YMCA

www.ymca.com

The largest nonprofit community service organization in America, working to meet the health and social service need of 18.9 million men, women, and children in 10,000 communities in the United States. Ys are for people of all faiths, races, abilities, ages, and incomes. The YMCA's strength is in the people it brings together.

YWCA

www.ywca.com

With more than 25 million members around the globe, the organization's mission is to "eliminate racism and empower women." The YWCA provides safe places for women and girls, builds strong girl leaders, and advocates for women's rights and civil rights in Congress.

Bibliography

About.com. "Stress Management Poll Results." http://stress.about. com/gi/pages/poll.htm?poll_id=3429098248&linkback (accessed October 4, 2004).

Aron, Arthur, et al. "Reward, Motivation, and Emotion Systems Associated With Early-Stage Intense Romantic Love." *Journal of Neurophysiology* 94: 327–337, 2006. May 31, 2005.

Fox, Annie, M.Ed. *The Teen Survival Guide to Dating and Relating: Real-World Advice for Teens on Guys, Girls, Growing up, and Getting Along.* Minneapolis: Free Spirit Publishing, 2005.

Goleman, Daniel. *Destructive Emotions: How Can We Overcome Them? A Scientific Dialogue with the Dalai Lama.* New York: Bantam Books, 2003.

Goleman, Daniel. *Emotional Intelligence: Why It Can Matter More Than IQ.* New York: Bantam Books, 1997.

Klein, Gary. *Sources of Power: How People Make Decisions.* Cambridge, MA: MIT Press, 1999.

LeDoux, Joseph. *The Emotional Brain: The Mysterious Underpinnings of Emotional Life.* New York: Simon and Schuster, 1998.

LeDoux, Joseph. *Synaptic Self: How Our Brains Become Who We Are.* New York: Penguin, 2003.

Levine, Mel, M.D. *A Mind at a Time.* New York: Simon and Schuster, 2002.

Maté, Gabor, M.D. *When Your Body Says No: Understanding the Stress-Disease Connection.* Indianapolis: Wiley, 2003.

National Sleep Foundation. "Teens & Sleep: Dozing Off in Class?" www.sleepfoundation.org/hottopics (accessed July 19, 2005).

Ratey, John J., M.D. *A User's Guide to the Brain: Perception, Attention, and the Four Theaters of the Brain.* New York: Vintage Books, 2002.

Sapolsky, Robert M. *Why Zebras Don't Get Ulcers: An Updated Guide to Stress, Stress-Related Diseases, and Coping.* New York: W. H. Freeman and Company, 1998.

Strauch, Barbara. *The Primal Teen: What the New Discoveries About the Teenage Brain Tell Us About Our Kids.* New York: Anchor, 2004.

Stress Institute at Roosevelt University. "Stress Institute Facts About Stress and Stress Management." www.roosevelt.edu/stress/facts.htm (accessed June 14, 2004).

Taylor, S.E., et al. "Biobehavioral Responses to Stress in Females: Tend-and-Befriend, Not Fight-or-Flight." *Psychological Review* 107: pp. 411–429. 2000.

Taylor, Shelley E. *The Tending Instinct: How Nurturing Is Essential to Who We Are and How We Live.* New York: Times Books, 2002.

Index

dating jobs family pressure
cliques homework identity tests
school bullying
friends

About the Authors

 **Annie Fox, M.Ed.,** is a writer, educator, and online advisor for teens. Annie's book *The Teen Survival Guide to Dating and Relating* (Free Spirit Publishing, 2005) is based on hundreds of teen email questions. See www.heyterra.com.

 **Ruth Kirschner** is a teacher, author, illustrator, and nationally produced, award-winning playwright who lives in San Francisco with her teenage daughter, Lucy.

Ruth and Annie are co-founders of "Stress and Ethics," a curriculum to help students understand the connection between stress response, temperament, and doing the right thing.

Other Great Books from Free Spirit

The Teen Survival Guide to Dating & Relating
Real-World Advice for Teens on Guys, Girls,
Growing Up, and Getting Along
by Annie Fox, M.Ed. (also known as Hey Terra!)
Online, the author is "Terra"—a wise person who's been around long enough to know plenty, but not so long that she's forgotten what it's like to be a teen. Based on hundreds of emails Annie has received, it gives readers the scoop on what matters most to teens: their feelings, looks, and decisions; boyfriends and girlfriends; sexuality; and much more. For ages 13 & up.
$15.95; 256 pp.; softcover; illus.; 7¼" x 9¼"

Life Lists for Teens
Tips, Steps, Hints, and How-Tos for Growing Up, Getting Along, Learning, and Having Fun
by Pamela Espeland
Everybody loves lists: making them, reading them, checking things off on them. In this book more than 200 powerful self-help lists cover topics ranging from health to cyberspace, school success to personal safety, friendship to fun. A 4-1-1 for tweens and teens, *Life Lists* is an inviting read and a ready source of guidance for all kinds of situations. For ages 11 & up.
$11.95; 272 pp.; softcover; 6" x 9"

Fighting Invisible Tigers
A Stress Management Guide for Teens, *Revised & Updated*
by Earl Hipp
Proven, practical advice for teens on coping with stress, being assertive, building relationships, taking risks, making decisions, dealing with fears, and more. For ages 11 & up.
$12.95; 160 pp.; softcover; illus.; 6" x 9"

Leader's Guide Available
For grades 6–12.
$19.95; 136 pp.; softcover; 8½" x 11"

Perfectionism
What's Bad About Being Too Good?
Revised and Updated Edition
by Miriam Adderholdt, Ph.D., and Jan Goldberg
This revised and updated edition includes new research and statistics on the causes and consequences of perfectionism, biographical sketches of famous perfectionists and risk takers, and resources for readers who want to know more. For ages 13 & up.
$12.95; 136 pp.; softcover; illus.; 6" x 9"

Boy v. Girl?

How Gender Shapes Who We Are, What We Want,
and How We Get Along

by George Abrahams, Ph.D., and Sheila Ahlbrand

This book invites young readers to examine gender roles and
stereotypes, overcome gender barriers, and be themselves.
Written for both boys and girls, it explores the issues and
examines the facts—about hormones, history, laws, and more.
It encourages readers to learn who they are, imagine what they
can be—and get past things that get in the way. For ages 10–15.

$14.95; 208 pp.; softcover; illus.; 7" x 9"

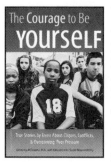

GLBTQ*

The Survival Guide for Queer & Questioning Teens

*Gay, Lesbian, Bisexual, Transgender, Questioning

by Kelly Huegel

A helpful look at the challenges and issues gay, lesbian, bisexual,
transgendered, and questioning teens face at school, at home,
and with friends. Recommended for any GLBTQ teen—and for
any straight friend, parent, teacher, or other adult who cares and
wants to understand. For ages 13 & up.

$15.95; 192 pp.; softcover; illus.; 6" x 9"

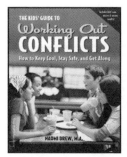

The Courage to Be Yourself

Edited by Al Desetta, M.A., with Educators for Social Responsibility

Cassandra is hassled for sitting with the "wrong" kids at lunch.
Dwan's own family taunts her for not being "black enough." Yet
they find the strength to face their conflicts and the courage to be
themselves. In 26 first-person stories, real teens write about their
lives with searing honesty. For ages 13 & up.

$13.95; 160 pp.; softcover; 6" x 9"

Leader's Guide Available

For teachers, social workers, and other adults who work with
youth in grades 7–12.

$24.95; 176 pp.; softcover; 8½" x 11"

The Kids' Guide to Working Out Conflicts

How to Keep Cool, Stay Safe, and Get Along

by Naomi Drew, M.A.

Proven ways to avoid conflict and defuse tough situations,
written by an expert on conflict resolution and peacemaking.
Includes tips and strategies for dealing with bullies, lessening
stress, and more. For ages 10–14.

$13.95; 160 pp.; softcover; illus.; 7" x 9"

Leader's Guide Available

For teachers, grades 5–9.

$21.95; 112 pp.; softcover; lay-flat binding; 8½" x 11"

More Than a Label
Why What You Wear or Who You're With
Doesn't Define Who You Are
by Aisha Muharrar

Techie. Geek. Freak. Goth. Jock. These are just a few of the labels teens endure every day. Written by a teen, this book empowers students to stand up for themselves, understand others, and consider how labels define, limit, stereotype, and hurt. The book goes beyond labels to consider related issues—including cliques, peer pressure, popularity, racism, self-esteem, sexism, and homophobia. For ages 13 & up.

$13.95; 152 pp.; softcover; illus.; 6" x 9"

When A Friend Dies
Revised & Updated Edition
by Marilyn E. Gootman, Ed.D.

Foreword by R.E.M. singer/songwriter Michael Stipe

The death of a friend is a wrenching event for anyone at any age. Teenagers especially need help coping with this painful loss. This sensitive book answers questions grieving teens often have, like "How should I be acting?" and "What if I can't handle my grief on my own?" The revised edition includes new quotes from teens, new resources, and new insights into losing a friend through violence. For ages 11 & up.

$9.95; 128 pp.; softcover; 5" x 7"

Fast, Friendly, and Easy to Use
www.freespirit.com

Browse the catalog

Info & extras

Many ways to search

Quick check-out

Stop in and see!

Our Web site makes it easy to find the positive, reliable resources you need to empower teens and kids of all ages.

For a fast and easy way to receive our practical tips, helpful information, and special offers, send your email address to upbeatnews@freespirit.com. View a sample letter and our privacy policy at www.freespirit.com.

1.800.735.7323 • fax 612.337.5050 • help4kids@freespirit.com